THE REVELS PLAYS

Former general editors
Clifford Leech
F. David Hoeniger
E. A. J. Honigmann
J. R. Mulryne
Eugene M. Waith

General editors
David Bevington, Richard Dutton, Alison Findlay
and Helen Ostovich

THE LADY'S TRIAL

Manchester University Press

THE REVELS PLAYS

THE REVELS PLAYS

THE LADY'S TRIAL

JOHN FORD

edited by Lisa Hopkins

MANCHESTER
UNIVERSITY PRESS

Manchester and New York

*distributed in the United States exclusively by
Palgrave Macmillan*

This edition published by Manchester University Press
Oxford Road, Manchester M13 9NR, UK
and Room 400, 175 Fifth Avenue, New York, NY 10010, USA
www.manchesteruniversitypress.co.uk

Distributed in the United States exclusively by
Palgrave Macmillan, 175 Fifth Avenue, New York,
NY 10010, USA

Distributed in Canada exclusively by
UBC Press, University of British Columbia, 2029 West Mall,
Vancouver, BC, Canada V6T 1Z2

British Library Cataloguing-in-Publication Data
A catalogue record for this book is available from the
British Library

Library of Congress Cataloging-in-Publication Data applied for

ISBN 978 0 7190 7895 8 hardback

First published 2011

Typeset
by Toppan Best-set Premedia Limited
Printed in Great Britain
by MPG Books Group in the UK

Contents

General Editors' Preface

Clifford Leech conceived of the Revels Plays as a series in the mid-1950s, modelling the project on the New Arden Shakespeare. The aim, as he wrote in 1958, was 'to apply to Shakespeare's predecessors, contemporaries, and successors the methods that are now used in Shakespeare's editing'. The plays chosen were to include well-known works from the early Tudor period to about 1700, as well as others less familiar but of literary and theatrical merit. 'The plays included', Leech wrote, 'should be such as to deserve and indeed demand performance'. We owe it to Clifford Leech that the idea became reality. He set the high standards of the series, ensuring that editors of individual volumes produced work of lasting merit, equally useful for teachers and students, theatre directors and actors. Clifford Leech remained General Editor until 1971, and was succeeded by F. David Hoeniger, who retired in 1985.

Ever since then, the Revels Plays have been under the direction of four or five general editors: initially David Bevington, E. A. J. Honigmann, J. R. Mulryne, and E. M. Waith. E. A. J. Honigmann retired in 2000 and was succeeded by Richard Dutton. E. M. Waith retired in 2003 and was succeeded by Alison Findlay and Helen Ostovich. J. R. Mulryne retired in 2010. Published originally by Methuen, the series is now published by the Manchester University Press, embodying essentially the same format, scholarly character, and high editorial standards of the series as first conceived. The series now concentrates on plays from the period 1558–1642. Some slight changes have been made: for example, starting in 1996 each index lists proper names and topics in the introduction and commentary, whereas earlier indexes focused only on words and phrases for which the commentary provided a gloss. Notes to the introduction are now placed together at the end, not at the foot of, the page. Collation and commentary notes continue, however, to appear on the relevant pages.

The introduction to each Revels play undertakes to offer, among other matters, a critical appraisal of the play's significant themes and images, its poetic and verbal fascinations, its historical context, its characteristics as a piece for the theatre, and its uses of the stage for which it was designed. Stage history is an important part of the story. In addition, the introduction presents as lucidly as possible the criteria for choice of copy-text and the editorial methods employed in presenting the play to a modern reader. The introduction also considers the play's date and, where relevant, its sources, together with its place in the work of the author and in the theatre of its time. If the play is by an author not previously represented in the series, a brief biography is provided.

The text of each Revels play, in accordance with established practice in the series, is edited afresh from the original text of best authority (in a few instances, texts), in modern spelling and punctuation and with speech headings that are consistent throughout. Elisions in the original are also silently regularised, except where metre would be affected by the change. Emendations, as distinguished from modernized spellings and punctuation, are introduced only in instances where error is patent or at least very probable, and where the corrected reading is persuasive. Act divisions are given only if they appear in the original, or if the structure of the play clearly points to them. Those act and scene divisions not in the original are provided in small type. Square brackets are also used for any other additions to, or changes in, the stage directions of the original.

Rather than provide a comprehensive and historical variorum collation, Revels Plays editions focus on those variants which require the critical attention of serious textual students. All departures of substance from the copy-text are listed, including any significant relineation and those changes in punctuation which involve to any degree a decision between alternative interpretations. The collation notes do not include such accidentals as turned letters or changes in the font. Additions to stage directions are not noted in the collations, since those additions are already made clear by the use of brackets. On the other hand, press corrections in the copy-text are duly collated, as based on a careful consultation of as many copies of the original edition or editions as are needed to ensure that the printing history of those originals is accurately reported. Of later emendations of the text by subsequent editors, only those are reported which still deserve attention as alternative readings.

One of the hallmarks of the Revels Plays is the thoroughness of their annotations. Besides explaining the meanings of difficult words and passages, the annotations provide commentary on customs or usage, on the text, on stage business – indeed, on anything that can be pertinent and helpful. On occasion, when long notes are required and are too lengthy to fit comfortably at the foot of the page below the text, they are printed at the end of the complete text.

Appendices are used to present any commendatory poems on the dramatist and play in question, documents about the play's reception and contemporary history, classical sources, casting analyses, music, and any other relevant material.

Each volume contains an index to the commentary, in which particular attention is drawn to meanings for words not listed in the OED, and (starting in 1996, as indicated above) an indexing of proper names and topics in the introduction and commentary.

Our hope is that plays edited in this fashion will promote further scholarly and theatrical investigation of one of the richest periods in theatrical history.

DAVID BEVINGTON
RICHARD DUTTON
ALISON FINDLAY
HELEN OSTOVICH

Acknowledgements

With thanks to Paulette Burchill of the Handsworth Historical Society; my colleagues Annaliese Connolly, Tom Rutter, Ana Maria Sanchez Arce and Matt Steggle; Carter Hailey; Ton Hoenselaars, Paul Franssen and Sabine Vanacker, who all wrestled valiantly with Fulgoso's speeches; Helen Nader; Katsuhiko Nogami; and Helen Ostovich for being a patient and exemplary general editor. Thanks too, as always, to Chris and Sam.

Abbreviations

EDITIONS AND TEXTUAL REFERENCES

Dyce   *The Works of John Ford*, notes by William Gifford rev.
            Alexander Dyce, 3 vols (London, 1869).
Gifford   *The Dramatic Works of John Ford*, ed. William Gifford,
            2 vols (London, 1827).
Keltie   John S. Keltie, ed., *The Works of the British Dramatists*
            (Edinburgh, 1870).
Nogami   Katsuhiko Nogami, 'A critical, modern-spelling edition
            of John Ford's *The Lady's Trial*' (PhD Diss., The
            Shakespeare Institute, 1989).
Q   *The Ladies Triall* (London, 1639).
Weber   *The Dramatic Works of John Ford*, ed. Henry Weber,
            2 vols (Edinburgh, 1811).

OTHER REFERENCES

Alemán   Mateo Alemán, *The Rogue: or the life of Guzman de
            Alfarache*, trans. James Mabbe (London: George Eld for
            Edward Blount, 1623) 4 vols.
Baskervill Charles Read Baskervill, *The Elizabethan Jig and Related
            Song Drama* [1929 (rpt) New York: Dover, 1965].
BH   John Ford, *The Broken Heart*, ed. T. J. B. Spencer
            (Manchester U. P., 1980).
Egan   Gabriel Egan, ' "Hearing or seeing a play?": evidence
            of early modern theatrical terminology', *Ben Jonson
            Journal* 8 (2001): 327–47.
EPT   *English Professional Theatre*, ed. Glynne Wickham,
            Herbert Berry and William Ingram (Cambridge U. P.,
            2000).
Gurr   Andrew Gurr, *The Shakespearean Playing Companies*
            (Oxford: The Clarendon P., 1996).

Hawkes   Terence Hawkes, *Meaning by Shakespeare* (London:
            Routledge, 1992).
McMaster   Juliet McMaster, 'Love, lust and sham: structural
            pattern in the plays of John Ford', *Renaissance Drama*
            new series 2 (1969): 157–66.
N&Q   *Notes and Queries.*
Sargeaunt   M. Joan Sargeaunt, *John Ford* (New York: Russell &
            Russell, 1966).
Steggle   Matthew Steggle, *Richard Brome: Place and Politics on
            the Caroline Stage* (Manchester U. P., 2004).
Stevens   David Stevens, 'The stagecraft of James Shirley',
            Educational Theatre Journal 29.4 (December 1977):
            493–516.
Tilley   Morris Palmer Tilley, *A Dictionary of the Proverbs in
            England in the Sixteenth and Seventeenth Centuries* (Ann
            Arbor: U. of Michigan P., 1950).
Wickham   Glynne Wickham, *English Professional Theatre, 1530–
            1660* (Cambridge U. P., 2000).

Works Cited

Jonson, Ben, *The Alchemist*, ed. F. H. Mares (London: Methuen, 1967).

Shakespeare is quoted from the Arden edition, and other dramatists from the Revels Plays editions where available.

Introduction

John Ford was baptised in Ilsington, Devon, on 12 April 1586.[1] He was the second son of Thomas Ford and his wife Elizabeth Popham, whose uncle was Sir John Popham, Lord Chief Justice, making John Ford the somewhat scapegrace great-nephew of a pre-eminently upright citizen just as the disgraced Levidolce is great-niece to the irreproachable Martino. Ford is usually identified as the 'John Ford Devon Gent.' who matriculated at Exeter College, Oxford, on 26 March 1601, before proceeding on 16 November 1602 to the Middle Temple, where Sir John Popham was treasurer and Ford's paternal cousin Thomas Ford already a member. Although there is no record that he was ever called to the bar, subsequent references to him in commendatory verses continue to associate him with the Middle Temple, although for the period between 1605 and 1608 he was officially expelled for not having paid his buttery bill. He may also have been in trouble in 1617, when the name 'John Ford' appears among those of forty members who protested against having to wear their lawyers' caps in hall, though there was another John Ford at the Middle Temple by then and it may have been he who was involved in this protest. He may also, or instead, have been the John Ford who was recorded as living somewhere near Holywell Street in 1619 or before.[2] Apart from these minor brushes with authority, little is known of Ford's life or career. In 1610 his father died and left him the relatively small sum of £10, perhaps an indication of parental disapproval, and in 1616 his elder brother died and left him £20. Nothing else is known of how he made his living, though it has been suggested that he may have acted as some sort of agent for the nobility, and, apart from an epigram addressed to him in 1640,[3] he effectively vanishes from sight after the publication of *The Lady's Trial*, when he would have been in his early fifties. There is no reason to suppose that his allusion to 'cruel Lycia' in his 1606 elegy *Fame's Memorial* was born of anything other than literary convention, and it seems unwise to attach much weight to Gifford's apparent uncovering of a 'local tradition' that Ford had ultimately retired to Devon and married.

The details of Ford's literary career are slightly easier to ascertain than those of his life, but are still full of puzzles. In 1606, when he would have been turning twenty, he published *Fame's Memorial*, an elegy on Charles Blount, earl of Devonshire and husband of Penelope Devereux, Sidney's Stella, and *Honour Triumphant*, a series of chivalric propositions apparently designed to accompany the festivities proposed for the visit of James I's brother-in-law, Christian IV of Denmark. Another elegy which appeared in 1612, this time for the Devon-born Master William Peter, is now generally agreed to be Ford's, after being briefly and notoriously assigned to Shakespeare.[4] A further pair of works appeared in 1613, the devotional poem *Christ's Bloody Sweat* and the moralising prose tract *The Golden Mean*. Both this and Ford's next work, *A Line of Life* (1620), show traces of the influence of Justus Lipsius and his English translator and populariser Sir John Stradling, who was Ford's cousin on his mother's side. Between these two morally minded treatises he also wrote an elegy on Sir Thomas Overbury in 1616 and may have added two 'characters' for the second edition of Overbury's poem 'A Wife' in 1614. Throughout his literary career he was also contributing commendatory verses to the works of authors including Barnabe Barnes, Webster, Massinger, Shirley and Brome, giving the impression of someone with a number of friends in the literary world. However, his own earliest certain foray into drama is *The Witch of Edmonton* (1621), on which he collaborated with Thomas Dekker and William Rowley, followed by *The Welsh Ambassador* in 1623 and *The Sun's Darling* in 1624, both also co-written with Dekker. In addition, Ford's name has been linked with greater or lesser degrees of certainty to a number of plays which are now lost, including *An Ill Beginning Has a Good End* (1613?) and *Beauty in a Trance*, which was acted at Court by the King's Men in 1630, as well as some further collaborative works with Dekker, *The Bristow Merchant*, *The Fairy Knight*, and *The Late Murther of the Son Upon the Mother* (on the last of which Webster also worked).

The last three of these all date from the 1620s, a period during which Ford may also have been involved in the writing of *The Spanish Gipsy* (1623), *The Laws of Candy* (1619–23), and *The Fair Maid of the Inn* (1626), and seems to have written a solo play, *The London Merchant*, of which it is just possible that some trace survives in a much later play of the same name by George Lillo.[5] Another possible palimpsest dating from the same period is Sir Robert Howard's *The Great Favourite: Or, The Duke of Lerma* (1668). This was attributed by Moseley to Henry Shirley, whose play *The Martyred Soldier* was published in 1638, but in 1940 Harbage confidently declared the ascription to Henry Shirley to be worthless and claimed instead that 'Ford I am sure is our man', since the play 'bears the stamp of Ford in its plot materials, its characters, and its style'.[6] Sensabaugh agreed with him, declaring that 'for ten years John Ford has been my constant companion, his voice becoming as familiar as that of an old friend's; and when I read *The Great Favourite* authentic accents fell on my ears',[7] while Robert Davril went so far as to say that 'la pièce telle que nous la possédons, taillée et modifiée par Howard, mérite même d'être incluse un jour dans une édition complète des oeuvres de Ford' (the play as we have it, shaped and changed by Howard, still deserves to be one day included in a complete edition of the works of Ford).[8] H. J. Oliver, however, declared that 'I have made a close study of *The Duke of Lerma* in an attempt to clinch the case for Ford but can only conclude that it must stop far short even of probabilty'.[9] One also needs to bear in mind, in any discussion of the authorship of the play, that Sir Robert Howard was extremely well read in Renaissance drama: a recent editor points out that Howard's first play *The Blind Lady* 'reveals his interest in, and knowledge of, the plays of his Elizabethan and Jacobean predecessors', and in particular that 'The Princess has similar traits of character to Calantha in *The Broken Heart*, and Caeca's servant Peter, "thou ingrateful piece of wise formality" . . . is often very like Ford's "wise formalitie" John a Water, Mayor of Cork, in *Perkin Warbeck*'.[10] Moreover, *The Surprisal* (1662) seems to show an intimate knowledge of *'Tis Pity She's a Whore*. Howard's apparent familiarity with Ford's work means that passages which seem to be parallel to passages in Ford need not necessarily have been written by Ford, since they could be skilled imitations, though lines like Maria's 'Come, sit down. See *Izabella*, / These flowers live without the sence of sorrowes' (4.1.12–13) do have the simplicity and cadence of Ford's verse at its very best, when it is conveying deliberately repressed emotion.

The Great Favourite includes a character named Velasco, and that name recurs in another anonymous play which can be more confidently attributed to Ford, *The Queen*, published in 1653 by Alexander Gough, who had acted in *The Lover's Melancholy* as a boy. This odd play revisits to a certain extent ideas first explored by Ford in *Honour Triumphant*, and has recently been read as informed by the Essex Rebellion, after which Ford's great-uncle Lord Chief Justice Popham served as judge at Essex's trial.[11] Ford's fame is, however, due almost entirely to the single-authored plays which are generally dated as starting from the second half of the 1620s and continuing through until the late 1630s, *The Lover's Melancholy*, *'Tis Pity She's a Whore*, *The Broken Heart*, *Love's Sacrifice*, *The Fancies Chaste and Noble*, and *The Lady's Trial*, after which he passes into silence.

THE DATE

The Lady's Trial is one of the very few Ford plays which can be securely dated. Sir Henry Herbert licensed it for performance on 3 May 1638, and it was entered in the Stationers' Register on 6 November 1638 before being published in 1639. Since *The Fancies Chaste and Noble* was printed in 1638 and must have been written between September 1635 (when Old Parr, who is referred to in it, came to Court) and May 1636, it seems reasonable to suppose that *The Lady's Trial* followed immediately after it, especially since Katsuhiko Nogami has pointed to a number of words and phrases which appear both here and in *The Fancies Chaste and Noble*,[12] although it is not impossible that *The Queen* intervened. None of Ford's other surviving single-authored plays can have done so, however, for they were all in print by 1634. Since the Prologue to *The Fancies* speaks of Ford being 'farre enough from home' (14), and since *The Fancies* must have been acted before 12 May 1636, because the title page announces that it was performed 'by the Queenes Maiesties Servants, At the Phoenix in Drury-lane' and after that date the Phoenix was closed because of plague,[13] it is not unreasonable to suppose Ford writing *The Fancies* in late 1635–36 and then departing on a journey of some sort, returning by 1638 to see *The Fancies* through the press. It seems, then, that we can date the composition of *The Lady's Trial* with some certainty to 1637–38.

SOURCES

In his doctoral thesis 'Ford's *Love's Sacrifice*, *The Lady's Trial*, and *The Queen*', Joe Andrew Sutfin suggested that 'It is unlikely that the play was written before 1632, the year of the publication in Spain of Bernal Diaz del Castillo's *Historia Verdadera de la Conquista de la Nueva Espana*', which he sees as the source for Guzman's mention of Cortés.[14] However, the story of Cortés was well known – he is for instance mentioned in Sir Walter Ralegh's *The Discoverie of the Large, Rich and Bewtiful Empyre of Guiana*[15] – and there seems no particular reason why the *Historia Verdadera* need have been the source of Ford's knowledge of it.

It is more profitable to look to literary sources, as indeed Guzman hints when he castigates those 'Not versed in literature' (3.1.9). Guzman himself seems to owe a debt to James Mabbe's translation of Mateo Alemán's *The Rogue*, first published in 1622 and reprinted as recently as 1634, where the eponymous hero is named Guzman de Alfarache, and is an illegitimate half-Genoese rogue who makes a great deal of parade of his allegedly noble ancestry and also spends a great deal of time describing his clothes.[16] The name Castanna is also found there, and a variant of the name Spinella occurs amongst the preliminary verses, of which the first is 'Ad Guzmanum de Alfarache, Vincentii Spinelli Epigramma'.[17] Another contributor of preliminary verses was Ben Jonson, and there are two sets, in Latin and English, signed 'I. F.'. There is nothing here to suggest possible authorship by John Ford, but it might conceivably be worth bearing in mind that the dramatist had a cousin of the same name, who also contributed occasional commendatory verses. It is perhaps worth noting that Mabbe, the translator, went to Spain in 1611 as secretary to Sir John Digby, who later became earl of Bristol (*The Rogue*, introduction, p. xxvi), cousin and friend of Sir Kenelm Digby, whose fictionalised autobiography *Private Memoirs: Loose Fantasies* appears to be a source for some of the names in *The Broken Heart*.[18] One section of *The Rogue* might particularly have caught Ford's attention, where we are told of how

> A Gentlewoman, that was young, faire, rich, and of a noble linage, being married to a Gentleman, in every respect equall unto her selfe, chanced within a short time after to become a widdow: who discreetly considering the dangers, whereinto by reason of her tender yeares, shee was like to fall, and what speeches the world is wont to cast out, through a too much aptnesse that men have to whisper and murmur strange tales; for every man judgeth so of things as they represent themselves to his imagination; and as hee is instructed by his private either fancy or affection; and taking notice of one onely action of this or that man or woman, it is a common practice among them, to varry their opinions thereupon, and give their severall censures. And yet not alwayes doe these tongues of theirs speake the truth; nor their judgements hit upon the right.[19]

The widow, then, finds herself in much the same situation as Spinella when Auria leaves Genoa. To avoid scandal, the widow

becomes engaged, but a rejected suitor unfairly makes her seem
unchaste, for which she takes revenge by killing him. The sense of
the vulnerability of a young woman to unjust report and the emphasis on the censoriousness of society both come close to *The Lady's
Trial*, though there the potentially tragic ending is averted by Auria's
careful management of the situation.

Nogami suggests another play, Beaumont and Fletcher's *Philaster*,
as a possible influence, in that Arethusa, like Spinella, is falsely
accused, but he essentially argues that the play does not really have
a source because in the dedication Ford calls it 'mine own'. He does
list some similarities to Massinger and Field's *The Fatal Dowry*,
but he also finds differences from it.[20] The principal similarities to
The Lady's Trial lie in the fact that many of Massinger and Field's
characters are motivated by poverty and debt and in Charalois's
resentment of Romont, the friend who alerts him to the probable
infidelity of the wife (a view shared by Charmi who ultimately
banishes Romont on the grounds that he had no warrant from the
state for what he did). There is also a form of trial of Beaumelle,
the adulterous wife. This is, however, cut short when Charalois kills
her, producing a denouement whose wholly tragic nature could
hardly be more different from the tonality of *The Lady's Tragedy*.

There are rather more similarities between *The Lady's Trial* and
Jonson's *The Alchemist*, and indeed Nogami, noting that 'Adurni
critises [Aurelio] for his "jealousy", "spleen" and "suspicious rage"
(IV.iii.39–50), all of which are Burtonian terms', points to the
number of usages which suggest that people are 'over-' something,
such as 'over-busy' (5.2.177) and suggests consequent affinities with
Jonson's brand of humoral comedy.[21] *The Alchemist*, like *The Lady's
Trial*, has some byplay about the Dutch and the Spanish, in the
shape of a group of exiled Dutch (and a little bit of spoken Dutch
at 2.4.7) and a fake Spanish don costume. One of those who wears
it, Surly, is said by Face to be proposing 'to make his batt'ry /
Upon our Doll, our castle, our Cinque Port'.[22] Ford could have taken the
'*chiauses*' of 2.1.200 of *The Lady's Trial* from the thrice-repeated
'*Chiaus*' of *The Alchemist* (1.2.26, 30, 35), and the term 'ging' for a
crowd, which Auria uses at 3.3.19, is also found in *The Alchemist*
(5.1.21). Sir Epicure Mammon courts Doll with promise of dainties
(4.1.154–66) as Guzman does Amoretta, and Surly in his Spanish
don disguise says '*beso las manos*' (4.3.21), a phrase also used by
Futelli (2.1.14). Particularly notable is the importance of bird
imagery in both texts. In *The Alchemist*, Face calls Doll 'my guinea-

bird' (4.1.38); Mammon says 'The Phoenix never knew a nobler death'; Ananias declares that 'The place, / It is become a cage of unclean birds' (5.3.46–7); Lovewit asks Face 'What's your med'cine, / To draw so many several sorts of wild-fowl?' (5.3.78–9); Subtle says to Doll 'My bird o'the night; we'll tickle it at the Pigeons' (5.4.89); and Face and Subtle are 'day-owls . . . birding in men's purses' (5.5.12). Bird imagery is particularly sustained in an exchange towards the end of the play:

> *Mammon.*   The whole nest are fled!
> *Lovewit.* What sort of birds were they?
> *Mammon.*   A kind of choughs,
>   Of thievish daws . . .
>
>   (5.5.58–60)

Finally, Lovewit says to Kastril of Dame Pliant, 'Here stands my dove: stoop at her, if you dare' (5.5.134) (indeed the Oxford edition spells Kastril Kestrel). Perhaps most suggestive is Face's comparison 'tame / As the poor black-birds were i' the great frost' (3.3.45–6), since tame blackbirds will also be referred to in *The Lady's Trial* (4.2.75).

The most obvious source of *The Lady's Trial*, however, is *Othello*. This is a play to which Ford recurs throughout his career, engaging with it so extensively that he has some claim to be considered as one of the first commentators on it. Both *'Tis Pity* and *Love's Sacrifice* feature a jealous husband (Soranzo, Caraffa) and an oddly dispassionate schemer (Vasques, D'Avalos), and the similarity in the case of *Love's Sacrifice* is increased by the fact that its heroine is called Bianca, the name of a secondary character in *Othello*. *The Fancies Chaste and Noble*, too, can be seen as influenced by *Othello*, since, like so much of Iago's gulling of *Othello*, this is a play which depends on the difference between how things really are and how they may be made to seem. In *The Lady's Trial*, the echoes are much more obvious: an older husband of a young wife is faced with two attacks simultaneously, one by the Turks and one on his wife's reputation, and in both plays the man the hero most trusts encourages him to believe the worst of his wife. Auria reacts very differently from Othello, and Aurelio's motive is a genuine if misguided belief in Spinella's infidelity rather than the 'motiveless malice' of Iago, but in both cases the question of proof and evidence proves crucial, and it is indeed perhaps *Othello*'s interest in this which was responsible for its particular appeal to the legally minded Ford.

Other texts may also have exerted an influence on Ford's. At
2.1.45 of *The Lady's Trial*, we hear of a personage called 'the Duchess
Infantasgo'. The name Infantasgo is the medieval form of the title
of the dukes of Infantado and occurs on the façade of the Infantado
Palace in Guadalajara, built by the second duke, Íñigo López de
Mendoza, in the early years of the sixteenth century.[23] Guadalajara
was also the birthplace of the notorious conquistador Nuño Beltrán
de Guzmán (Guadalajara in Mexico was so named in honour of
this), which may explain why at 2.1.46–9 Guzman speaks of

> Our cloak whose cape is
> Larded with pearls, which the Indian caciques
> Presented to our countryman De Cortez
> For ransom of his life

This comes straight after he has mentioned 'The Duchess
Infantasgo', at 2.1.45.

The name Infantasgo is rarely found in English writing of this
period, and the other locations in which it occurs are of interest.
The first to consider, given the play's interest in the Netherlands
and its inclusion of a Dutch character, is Edward Grimeston's 1608
continuation of Jean François Le Petit's *A generall historie of the
Netherlands With the genealogie and memorable acts of the Earls of
Holland, Zeeland, and west-Friseland*, where the Duke of Infantasgo
is mentioned in passing as part of the reception party for the French
princess Elisabeth de Valois. However, apart from one or two mentions of the family of Caraffa, who are also mentioned in Ford's play
Love's Sacrifice, and of a character called Carlo Spinella, there is
nothing in this text to suggest that Ford might have used it as a
source. A different tale emerges, though, with three other works
which mention the Duke of Infantasgo.

The first of these is Thomas Scott's *Sir Walter Raleighs Ghost, or
Englands forewarner Discouering a secret consultation, newly holden in
the Court of Spaine*, published at Utrecht in 1626. This opens with
a discussion of 'Currants, Gazettas, Pasquils, and the like', recalling
the reference in *The Lady's Trial* to corantos and gazettes (1.1.6),
and then goes on to discuss a vision experienced by Count Gondomar
shortly after a meeting whose personnel included the Duke of
Infantasgo and the Duke of Lerma. It also includes another term
found in *The Lady's Trial*, pistolets,[24] and has much praise for Essex,
a figure in whom Ford was very interested. Moreover, Ford's interest in Ralegh, whom he discusses in *A Line of Life* and whose trial

had been presided over by his great-uncle Sir John Popham, might well have drawn this work to his attention.

Secondly Richard Jones's *The Booke of Honor and Armes*, printed in 1590 by a different Richard Jones, has at the start of its Fourth Book a long discussion of the true nature of nobility, a subject which greatly interested Ford, and concludes, as Ford himself might well have done, that 'naturall Nobilitie mixed with Vertue is most true and perfect'. It also mentions by name John Wolley, whose granddaughter Mary Wyrley is, along with her husband, the dedicatee of *The Lady's Trial*, as well as including 'Don Inigo Lopez de Mendoza, Duke of Infantasgo' amongst the Knights of the Golden Fleece, in a list which goes on to include 'Antonio Doria' and 'Don Francisco Fernandes d'Auolos', another name familiar from Ford,[25] since D'Avalos is the villain of *Love's Sacrifice*. This text also contains a discussion of whether a king may challenge an emperor to combat, which might well have interested Ford, since he touches on a similar question in *Perkin Warbeck*.

Most interesting of all, though, is Anthony Copley's *Wits, Fittes and Fancies Fronted and entermedled with presidentes of honour and wisdome* (1595), which was also printed by the Richard Jones who was the printer of *The Booke of Honor* (and presumably written before 1595, since the preface to the gentlemen readers refers to Spenser as still alive). In *Wits, Fittes and Fancies* one of the several mentions of the Duke of Infantasgo occurs a line below the unusual word 'Copesmate', which is also found in *The Lady's Trial*, while another term from *The Lady's Trial*, 'butter-box', occurs later on. Ford could also have found here the name Gusman, as well as Velasco, which he used in *The Queen*, and a friar called Bonadventure, like the one in *'Tis Pity She's a Whore*. *Wits, Fittes and Fancies* also contains an apophthegm which Ford might have remembered, 'better is ciuill strangenesse, than rude familiarity';[26] in *The Lady's Trial*, Malfato complains,

> Sure state and ceremony
> Inhabit here; like strangers, we shall wait
> Formality of entertainment. Cousin,
> Let us return. 'Tis paltry.

(5.2.7–10)

Copley himself was most famous for his involvement in the Bye Plot, and the Bye Plot is something to which Ford seems to refer openly in the prologue to *The Lover's Melancholy*, ll. 13–16:

For your parts, gentlemen, to quit his pains,
Yet you will please that, as you meet with strains
Of lighter mixtures, but to cast your eye
Rather upon the main than on the bye.

It was Copley who implicated Ralegh,[27] to whom Ford refers frequently in his early verse. When convicted, Copley hoped for trial
by combat.[28] Finally, Copley declared that there was 'another
matter . . . of a man toward my Lord Mordant who (as Mr Watson
told me) uttered certayne speaches importing danger to ther person
of my lord Cecill',[29] and Lord Mordaunt was the dedicatee of 'Tis
Pity She's a Whore.

Anthony Copley came from a family which would have been of
interest to Ford in a number of ways. His father, Thomas Copley,
'suddenly converted to Catholicism in 1563 and later went into
exile'.[30] His mother, Catherine Luttrell, was the daughter of Sir John
Luttrell of Dunster Castle (Copley's younger brother John, who
eventually converted to Protestantism, used the alias of Luttrell).
Andrew Boyle notes that the marriage between Anthony Copley's
parents was arranged by the Earl of Arundel, who had bought the
wardship of Catherine Luttrell and both her sisters. Arundel was
one of the co-dedicatees of Ford's early work Honour Triumphant,
and Boyle notes that 'It is possible that the first translator of Lipsius
into English, Sir John Stradling, may have spent his formative years
under Arundel's influence, as his family were closely associated with
the Earl';[31] John Stradling was a cousin of John Ford, since Ford's
mother Elizabeth Popham was the great-granddaughter of Sir
Edward Stradling. (The Pophams were notoriously interested in
their ancestry – Catherine Grace Canino notes that 'the Popham
family tree reached impressively back to Noah who, according to
Genesis, was a direct descendant of Adam and Eve'.)[32] Further,
Copley's sister was married to a member of the Gage family, who
had close kinship ties with the Stradlings. Another member of the
Luttrell family, Thomas Luttrell of Dunster Castle, sheriff of
Somerset, was married in 1621 to Ford's cousin Jane Popham,
daughter of Sir Francis Popham of Littlecote, and Catherine
Luttrell's sister Mary married Henry Shirley of Mapledurham, a
Catholic and a cousin of Thomas Copley, who also had family con-
nections with Ford through his Stradling relations, and Hugh
Luttrell's widow married Edward Stradling.[33] It is, therefore, intrigu-
ing that the quarto copy of The Lady's Trial now in Yale University

Library has inscribed on its title page the name of Narcissus Luttrell (1657–1732), a member of a junior branch of the family, together with the record that he gave 8*d* for it.

The Luttrells, in turn, were connected with the Mohuns, another family probably known to Ford. Sir H. C. Maxwell Lyte, the historian of the two families, notes that 'In 1374, Lady de Mohun arranged to sell the reversion of the castle and manor of Dunster, the manors of Minehead and Kilton, and the hundred of Carhampton to Lady Elizabeth Luttrell, a widow of noble birth'.[34] It was to Catherine, Lady Mohun, wife of Warwick Mohun, baron of Okehampton, that Alexander Gough dedicated *The Queen*, a play which was published anonymously during the Interregnum but is almost certainly by Ford. Lady Mohun, like some of Ford's dedicatees, was a known Catholic (in the reign of Charles II, she was deprived of the care of her children because of it), and both her father-in-law and grandfather-in-law, John Mohun (d. 1641) and Reynold Mohun, had, like Ford, attended Exeter College, Oxford, and the Middle Temple. Another sign of a possible connection is that Sir Aston Cokain, a relative of the Mohuns, used the name Spinella for the heroine of his 1669 *The Tragedy of Ovid* and contributed commendatory verses to Massinger's *The Maid of Honour* (1632), which contains a character named Adorni. In the reference to the 'Duke of Infantasgo', then, we may glimpse a pointer not only to what Ford has been reading but also, perhaps, to who had been reading Ford.

THE SETTING

Almost the first thing we are told about *The Lady's Trial* is that it is set in Genoa. This was a city with a rather unsavoury reputation. In *The Rogue*, where Genoa figures prominently, a marginal note observes that 'The proudest, and hardest-hearted people in Italy, are your Genoveses';[35] in Marston's *The Malcontent*, Malevole declares that 'I would sooner leave my lady singled in a bordello than in the Genoa palace',[36] a vision which might well be seen as informing Aurelio's readiness to believe the worst of Spinella when he finds her alone in a room in Genoa. Ford might also have been aware of the depiction of Genoa in Fynes Moryson's *Itinerary*; Moryson was the secretary of Charles Blount, earl of Devonshire, whose death was the subject of Ford's early elegy *Fame's Memorial*, and had dedicated the *Itinerary* to the Earl of Pembroke, who was the dedicatee of Ford's *Christ's Bloody Sweat* and, with his brother, one of the four dedicatees of his *Honour Triumphant*. From Moryson's work he could have learned of Genoa's possession of Corsica, since Moryson in his discussion of Genoa refers to 'the hereditary quarrells betweene that Citty, and the Dukes of Florence, in regard that Genoa still keepeth the Forte of Sorezana of old belonging to the Citty of Florence and the Iland Corsica of old subiect to the Citty of Pisa'. Moryson says much of the greatness of Andrea d'Auria (usually better known as Andrea Doria): 'The said Andrea d'Auria is much praised of the Italians, that he not only freed his Country from all subiection, but also hauing that power yet forbore to inuade the liberty thereof himself'. Finally, Moryson could have provided the suggestion for the presence of a Spaniard and a Dutchman in Genoa, since he mentions the considerable Spanish involvement in Genoese affairs and the protection the Spanish gave to D'Auria and says 'The Duke being head of the Common Wealth is chosen for two yeares, during which tyme he liues in the publike Palace, and hath 300 Dutchmen for the guarde of his body'. Moryson also mentions 'the Familyes Adorni and Fregosi',[37] but Adorno was a name Ford might have encountered in any case, since the husband of St Catherine of Genoa was Giuliano Adorno, and religious imagery seems to be on Ford's mind in this play: Adurni speaks of 'that saint / To whom I vow myself' (2.4.42–3), a language picked up when Malfato speaks of Levidolce's 'conversion' (5.2.217) and Auria calls it a 'holy day' (5.2.221).

The two most important things about the Genoa which Ford depicts, though, are that it is in the political ambit of the dukes of Florence (as is also the case in *The Fancies Chaste and Noble*, which is set in Siena) and at war with the Turks, who, as so generally in English literature of the period, represent an absolute evil, as is seen in *The Golden Mean* when the putative traveller to Constantinople actually arrives:

> and, what is the worst of these adventures, if hee obtaine the scope of his desires, and arrive even to the furthest of his journey, yet shall he there finde a Turke that is Emperour, cruell in nature, boundlesse in command, faithlesse of truth, treacherous, and full of the bloud of Christians.

Later in *The Golden Mean*, Turks are even more summarily dismissed as 'the common enemie of God and Truth, the *Turke*',[38] while in *Christ's Bloody Sweat* we read of how

>   as some *Christian* Marchant by a Turke
> Surprisd, and chayn'd, is made a gally-slave,
> Whipt every day, and forc't to toyle and worke,
> Consum'd with griefe, still living in a grave,
>   Untill some one more strong, doth free his payne,
>   And set's him in his wonted state agayne:
>
> So men, that in a maze of dreadfull errour
> Did treade the pathes of miseries and woe,
> Bound by that Turke the *Devill*, slav'd to that terror
> Of condemnation, labour'd to and fro.[39]

In *The Lady's Trial*, the ever-present danger of the Turks has even infected vocabularies, so that Fulgoso finds the Turkish word '*chi-auses*' (2.1.200) come naturally to his lips.

The references to the Turks in *The Lady's Trial* partly reflect a political reality but also work to reinforce the similarities with *Othello*. The sea-war which forms the play's background may also account for the high amount of nautical imagery in this play: we hear of 'cabins' (3.3.23) and 'beverage and biscuit' (1.1.27), of 'brace' (3.3.22), which is the turn of a sail, and also of other sails such as the top and topgallant (2.1.54) and the luff (4.2.191). Aurelio tells Auria that 'Thou art near / Already on a shipwreck' (1.1.144–5), and Fulgoso figures disaster in specifically nautical terms when he says that they will 'eat and drink, and squander, / Till all do split again' (2.1.203–4), echoing *The Tempest* where 'split' is the term used for the ship breaking up. Finally, Auria, who during the course of the play has been appointed Genoa's admiral, says,

> After distress at sea, the danger's o'er;
> Safety and welcomes better taste ashore.
>
>   (5.2.255–6)

This interest in the language of ships is a new thing in Ford, not found in his earlier plays or non-dramatic works, where references to ships and sailing tend to be strictly metaphorical, as in *Linea Vitae: A Line of Life* where we find 'So in this Ship of our mortalitie, howsoever wee limit our courses, or are suited in any fortune of prosperitie or lownesse, in this great Sea of the World'.[40]

It is tempting to relate these new, more concrete uses to the statement in the prologue to *The Fancies Chaste and Noble* that Ford is 'farre enough from home'. (Obviously any suggestions about where he might have travelled to can be based only on speculation, but his fellow-dramatist James Shirley is known to have been in Ireland

from 1636 to 1640, and Shirley wrote commendatory verses for
Love's Sacrifice.) Equally, though, it might be significant that Ford
wrote commendatory verses for Captain Charles Saltonstall's *The
Navigator*, published in 1636, which was dedicated to Ford's own
earlier dedicatee the earl of Arundel (Saltonstall was the brother of
the poet and translator Wye Saltonstall, who may have been at
Gray's Inn in the early 1620s),[41] and that work contains references
to both 'top-gallant-sayle' and 'aluffe'.[42] It may also be worth noting
that Ford was connected through the Stradlings with Sir Thomas
Button, the explorer of Hudson Bay,[43] and it was Ford's great-uncle
on his mother's side, Lord Chief Justice Sir John Popham, who had
presided over the trial of another famous seafarer, Sir Walter Ralegh.
A Captain George Popham, who may well have been another relative, gave details of the Guiana coastline to Robert Dudley's expedi-
tion and brought back news about El Dorado,[44] and Emery
Molyneux's Globe, which was based on Drake's voyage, 'was sent
to London to be preserved at Drake's favourite institution, the
Middle Temple', which Ford attended.[45] He may, therefore, have
had a general interest in the sea traceable perhaps in part to his
family and his surroundings, or it may simply have been that the
name of Andrea Doria inevitably caused his imagination to run
along maritime lines.

THE PLAY

The Lady's Trial tells a number of intertwined stories, linked by a
common concern with the behaviour of women. The main plot
centres on the marriage of the Genoese soldier and sailor Auria and
his new young wife Spinella, who have married shortly before the
play begins, and the play opens with two young wits, Piero and
Futelli, discussing the fact that no sooner have they married than
Auria is preparing to depart to fight the Turks. Auria himself then
enters with Adurni, a nobleman of Genoa, and, after briefly taking
leave of Adurni, Piero, and Futelli, he is joined by Spinella, her sister
Castanna and his own uncle Trelcatio, to whose care he has con-
fided Spinella for the duration of his absence. After a long scene of
parting in which Spinella expresses her concern about what may
happen to him, she, Castanna, and Trelcatio leave and Auria says
his final farewell, this time to his close friend Aurelio, to whom he
confides that the reason for his departure is that his already difficult
financial situation has been made even worse by his marriage.

Aurelio first reproaches him for not having been frank about this and then warns him that Spinella is bound to be tempted to indiscretion during his absence, but Auria indignantly dismisses this inisinuation and departs.

The next scene introduces the sub-plots. First, Adurni and Futelli are discussing Levidolce, a young Genoese divorceé who has been having an affair with Adurni but has now transferred her affections to Malfato. They are joined by Piero and together Piero and Futelli tell Adurni about a young, affected girl called Amoretta (who we later discover has a marked lisp) and their scheme for curing her of her folly, which involves the braggadocio soldiers Fulgoso and Guzman. Although the audience does not know it at this stage, the characters in both these sub-plots are linked to the main plot: Malfato is the cousin of Spinella and Castanna, and Amoretta is the daughter of Trelcatio and hence the cousin of Auria. Moreover, Fulgoso and Guzman are Dutch and Spanish respectively, so their squabble over Amoretta mirrors the conflict between the United Provinces of the Netherlands and their Spanish invaders, reminding the audience of the wartime background of the play as a whole. The three subsequent scenes stay with these two strands: first we see Malfato, in company with Aurelio, receive Levidolce's love-letter, which he regards as an insult; next Fulgoso and Guzman discuss their respective approaches to the conquest of Amoretta, which they approach as if it were a military campaign; and finally we meet Levidolce herself, who is being reproached by her uncle Martino for her wanton ways. He breaks off when Trelcatio arrives to bring news that Auria has defeated the Turks.

We now return to the main plot. Adurni, who has decided to take advantage of Auria's absence to court Spinella, has invited her and Castanna to his house, along with Piero, Futelli and Amoretta. While the others are admiring works of art, he isolates Spinella in a room where a song incites her to love. Spinella indignantly refuses his advances, but while she is doing so Aurelio bursts in on them and assumes the worst. Spinella flees and Aurelio vows to tell Auria what he thinks he has discovered.

A new character now enters the play in the shape of Benazzi, a rough and ragged soldier who is in fact the divorced first husband of Levidolce, who recognises him instantly but does not reveal that she has done so. Significantly, she first sees him from the balcony, just as in 'Tis Pity She's a Whore we learn of Annabella's repentance while she is on the balcony, suggesting that this literal elevation is the sign of a moral elevation. Although we do not know it yet, Benazzi has in fact been away fighting under Auria, who in the next scene also returns and is heaped with honours. As soon as he is alone with Aurelio, however, Auria reveals his private agony over Spinella's disappearance, and the two men all but quarrel over Aurelio's insistence that this signifies her guilt. Castanna arrives, but says she has no knowledge of Spinella's whereabouts, which Aurelio again construes as a bad sign.

The suspense over Spinella's disappearance continues as the next scene returns to the Benazzi/Levidolce sub-plot. Benazzi meets Levidolce by prior arrangement and, still unaware that she has recognised him, agrees to kill Malfato and Adurni to avenge their rejections of her and to win her love. We then move to Malfato's house and discover that this is where Spinella has taken refuge. Malfato reveals that he has always loved her and was prevented from asking for her hand in marriage only by a scruple about the closeness of their kinship, but Spinella is either genuinely too distracted to understand what he has said or tactfully pretends to be so. They are joined by Castanna, who brings news that Auria has returned and has expressed his trust in Spinella, but we are still unclear what Spinella means to do.

The next scene returns to the story of Amoretta, who is courted at some length by both Fulgoso and Guzman. Prompted by Piero and Futelli, she finally sees through them and begins to renounce her pretensions to grandeur. This is followed by an apparently pre-arranged meeting between Auria, Aurelio, and Adurni to discuss the situation; during the meeting, Auria seems to form a plan, but the audience is not told what it is. We then return to the Benazzi/Levidolce story: they inform Martino of their marriage and Martino berates them, but Levidolce privately informs him of Benazzi's identity and he is appeased. Benazzi, however, leaves to fulfil his previous commitment to kill Malfato and Adurni, with Martino and Levidolce in pursuit.

The denouement of all three plots takes place at Trelcatio's house. Auria arrives and stages a form of trial of Spinella, who at first defends herself vigorously but then faints. Auria seizes on this as proof of her innocence, rather as the Friar in *Much Ado About Nothing* similarly interprets Hero's faint, and proposes that to clear the air Adurni should marry Castanna. Benazzi bursts in, but Auria disarms him and announces that he knows him for a valiant soldier. Levidolce reveals that she knew all along who he was and Trelcatio announces that Amoretta will marry Piero. Auria, who has been rewarded by the state with the governorship of Corsica, promises to find employment for Piero and Futelli, and the play ends with everyone happy.

Although the sailing metaphors may be a new feature in Ford's writing, it has often been remarked that *The Lady's Trial* has features in common with Ford's other plays. Lois E. Bueler, for instance, suggests that

> In the last and best of his tragicomedies, *The Lady's Trial* (published in 1639), John Ford brings to schematic and dramatic perfection a structural pattern that is also used with varied success in his three tragedies – *The Broken Heart*, *Love's Sacrifice*, and *'Tis Pity She's a Whore* (all published in 1633). The plots of all four plays concern the moral testing of a woman. Ford's structural pattern involves elaborate role-splitting among the male participants in the text, a splitting designed to make complex psychological relationships dramatically accessible.[46]

Brian Opie sees *The Lady's Trial* as being closely linked with *Love's Sacrifice*, with both focusing on the forgiveness and rehabilitation of erring women,[47] while Dorothy M. Farr sees both *The Fancies* and *The Lady's Trial* as harking back to the themes and structure of domestic tragedy.[48] One might well note that Ithocles in *The Broken Heart* offers a comment very pertinent to the way the relationship between Auria and Aurelio comes under strain on the marriage of the former:

> Friendship, though it cease not
> In marriage, yet is oft at less command
> Than when a single freedom can dispose it.
>
> (4.3.100–2)

Equally one could note that the stress on the importance of uncles in *The Lady's Trial* is also found in *The Lover's Melancholy*, *'Tis Pity She's a Whore*, and *The Fancies Chaste and Noble*, while in *Fame's Memorial* the mention of an uncle makes an unusual detail in an otherwise familiar image of civil war: 'The sonne against the Father long oppos'd, / The Unkle with the nephew at debate'.[49]

Equally characteristic is the play's interest in posthumous reputation and in the tombs which record it. In *'Tis Pity She's a Whore* the lovers swear by their mother's grave, and in *Love's Sacrifice* Fernando arises out of a tomb. This is also something which can be seen in Ford's early prose and poetry, which evinces a generally stoical attitude in which worldly success is either unattainable or ultimately ephemeral and what matters most is the image that constitutes one's legacy; indeed the title of Ford's first known work is *Fame's Memorial.* In *The Lady's Trial*, there is a sustained interest in epitaphs and what they may say. Certainly this idea seems to lie behind Auria's injunction to Spinella that she should act in such a way that 'no remembrance may impeach thy rest' (1.1.114), and his view that

> A woman's virtue in her lifetime writes
> The epitaph all covet on their tombs.
>
> (1.1.121–2)

Spinella tells Adurni 'be gentler to your fame / By purchase of a life to grace your story' (2.4.30–1), and later Adurni hopes for 'A memorable mention' (4.3.82). In this sense, Ford could be said to be ending where he began.

There are, however, other sustained image patterns which are not so familar. It is ironically fitting that, in a play introduced by a Mr Bird, birds should figure strongly. Adurni speaks to Auria of 'Your resolution, winged with thoughts so constant' (1.1.42). Futelli and Piero develop an extended avian metaphor:

> *Futelli.*   A brace of kestrels,
>   That fluttered, sir, about this lovely game,
>   Your daughter; but they durst not give the souse
>   And so took hedge.
> *Piero.*   Mere haggards, buzzards, kites.
>
> (4.2.187–90)

And Auria figures himself as a bird when he says

> In all my flight of vanity and giddiness,
> When scarce the wings of my excess were fledged,
> When a distemperature of youthful heat
> Might have excused disorder and ambition,
> Even then, and so from thence till now the down
> Of softness is exchanged for plumes of age
> Confirmed and hardened . . .
>
> (4.3.22–8)

In many of Ford's plays, we have a sense of the difficulties and constraints of living in a small community: this is evident in *The Witch of Edmonton*, and so strongly marked in *'Tis Pity She's a Whore* that Verna Foster has termed it a 'city tragedy'.[50] In *The Lady's Trial*, bird imagery provides a rare glimpse of freedom amidst the social constraints of Genoa.

In marked contrast to the idea of flight is the even more persistent use of images drawn from accounting. Spinella laments 'How am I left then to account with griefs' (1.1.83); Adurni speaks of 'a kind of compliment / Scarce entered to the times' (1.2.98–9), where 'entered' seems to mean 'stored up to the credit of', and tells his followers that they 'coin a humour' (1.2.100); Auria speaks of 'Accounts scored on the tally of my vengeance' (3.3.99) and Adurni tells Aurelio to

> be accountant
> Whither, with all the eagerness of spleen
> Or a suspicious rage can plead, thou hast
> Enforced the likelihood of scandal.

(4.3.48–51)

Finally, Adurni warns,

> he amongst you
> Who calls an even reckoning shall meet
> An even accountant.

(5.2.132–4)

This recurring language ensures that we remember that it was Auria's poverty which first set the events of the play in motion, and that financial uncertainty governs the actions of Futelli, Piero and Benazzi throughout.

The play is also clearly influenced by Ford's own legal training. Subha Mukherji observes that

> False trials in early modern drama occur in the fertile intermediate space between actual legal procedure and general thinking about ways of knowing, driven as they are by the impulse to ascertain or discover. This drive towards truth urges on the distinct trials that two husbands put their wives through in Massinger's *The Picture* (1629) and Ford's *The Lady's Trial* (1638).

She argues that

> Ford, legally trained but also informed in the literary traditions, makes deft use of the interface of forensic and dramatic languages and modes of proof. Auria's definition of probability entails the deliberate and deliberative generation of uncertainty, which goes against the grain of the probability he is ostensibly trying to prove. To establish the unlikeliness of Spinella's guilt and correct disbelief, he torments her through a judicial plot built on a rhetorical elaboration of suspicion.[51]

Certainly the play is full of legal language. Spinella says,

> Let me appear,
> Or mine own lawyer, or in open court
> (Like some forsaken client) in my suit
> Be cast for want of honest plea.

$$(2.4.97{-}100)$$

Adurni declares 'I make my judge my jury' (4.3.48) and speaks of
'My commission on mine error' (4.3.95), and the Epilogue is entirely
structured round the idea of a sitting:

> The court's on rising; 'tis too late
> To wish the lady in her fate
> Of trial now more fortunate.
> A verdict in the jury's breast
> Will be given up anon at least;
> Till then 'tis fit we hope the best.
> Else if there can be any stay,
> Next sitting without more delay,
> We will expect a gentle day.

James Howe notes that 'The vocabulary of law dominates the language of the main plot, and incidents in this plot take the form of
the progressing stages of legal proceedings', and suggests that 'It is
not the actual guilt or innocence of Spinella that is the subject of
the last scene, even though of all the play's scenes this one bears the
closest resemblance to an actual "trial." Rather, its subject is the
thematic material of the play: what one learns about abstract values
from trying Spinella'.[52] One could equally say that what the play is
most interested in is in fact the whole idea of proof, which is in turn
another sign of its interest in *Othello*.

Howe also suggests that 'realism of character and event were not
Ford's goals',[53] and the prevalence of split lines in the play does
sometimes have the effect of making the characters sound as if they
speak seamlessly rather than individually. Nevertheless, much of the
interest of *The Lady's Trial* lies in its delicately sketched characters.
As I have already suggested, Auria, the play's hero, is to some extent
a variation on Othello. Like Othello, Auria is a soldier, something
emphasised when he hears the word 'Matter?' (5.2.183), signalling
the start of a quarrel, and suddenly snaps to alertness; like Othello,
he is older than his wife; like Othello, he is a successful war leader
who finds himself posted to an island in the Mediterranean by the
government of an Italian city-state. Unlike Othello, however, he

never seems to entertain any serious doubts about his wife's fidelity; in this respect, it is as if the plot of *Othello* were being invoked only in order that we might recognise the differences from it.

Yet, despite his apparent faith in Spinella, Auria does subject her to a trial, however private and informal. Subha Mukherji asks 'what was Auria's motive? Why does he put her through it?'.[54] Perhaps a partial answer is provided in *The Fancies Chaste and Noble*, where Livio says 'Be now my Sister, stand a triall bravely' (3.3.154), and there is a suggested logic too in Martino's instruction to Levidolce,

> Accuse yourself, be your own jury, judge
> And executioner. I make no sport
> Of my vexation.
>
> (2.2.81–3)

Martino's implicit equation of trials with sport suggests, quite simply, that the process has a kind of entertainment value, and so perhaps it had for an audience which was indeed often full of lawyers.[55] Auria's wish to demonstrate Spinella's innocence rather than simply believe in it also has other overtones. It bespeaks a concern with appearances as well as reality which again testifies to the pressure of living in a small society. By his action, Auria does not merely cement his own relationship with Spinella; he also secures her position in society. In this, his last play, Ford develops the concern with the possible discrepancy between image and reality already apparent in *The Fancies Chaste and Noble* and deftly and sensitively sketches dramatic characters who are possessed both of a convincing sense of private subjectivity and also of a public persona.

Spinella's motives seem simpler: she loves Auria, and is determined to maintain her innocence and fight for her marriage. Nevertheless, there is a certain ambiguity in the representation of Spinella. She takes her name from a jewel, the spinel, and Ford is very interested in the language of jewels. In *Fame's Memorial* we are told that 'Jewell's being had for Jewel's are not know'n';[56] in *The Broken Heart*, Penthea figures her youth, her fame and her brother all as jewels (3.5.49–69); in *Love's Sacrifice*, the Duke boasts that

> I am a monarch of felicity,
> Proud in a pair of jewels rich and beautiful:
> A perfect friend, a wife above compare.[57]

Most notably, in *The Fancies Chaste and Noble* the Marquis discusses knowledge of jewels:

> *Octavio.* But for this grace (Madam) I will lay open
>   Before your judgements which I know can rate 'em,
>   A Cabinet of Jewels, rich and lively,
>   The world can shew none goodlier; those I prize
>   Deare as my life. – Nephew.
> *Troylo-Savelli.*   Sir, I obey you.   *Exit.*
> *Flavia.* Jewels, my Lord?
> *Octavio.* No strangers eye ere view'd them,
>   Unlesse your Brother Romanello haply
>   Was wo'd unto a sight for his approvement;
>   No more.
> *Romanello.* Not I, I doe protest. I hope Sir
>   You cannot thinke I am a lapidarie –
>   I skill in Jewels?
> *Octavio.*   'Tis a proper quality
>   For any Gentleman; your other friends
>   May be are not so coy.
> *Julio.*   Who, they? They know not
>   A *Topaze* from an *Opall.*
> *Camillo.*   We are ignorant
>   In gems which are not common.

(5.3.35–51)

Julio and Camillo might, therefore, have been baffled by a spinel, the gem from which Spinella derives her name, for it is an unusual gem, being most frequently red in colour (although blue is also not uncommon) but rather less precious than a ruby: a good woman may be above the price of rubies, but a spinel is not quite a ruby, although Peter Martyr considers spinels equivalent in price to balas rubies.[58] Indeed the play comes close to incriminating Spinella at times, first when she is heard of losing money gambling, and second when she is found with Adurni, an episode of which Thelma Greenfield observes that

> In his minor plays, Ford does little more than make his ladies act so as to look as bad as possible: in *Fancies Chaste and Noble* what is going on in that peculiar school for young ladies? In *The Lady's Trial* how can maligned Spinella be caught in one man's bedroom and hide in another man's house and still be innocent; and how can her husband's honor dishonor her?[59]

Even Spinella's attempt to defend herself becomes somehow suspect, when Auria says 'High and peremptory! The confidence is masculine' (5.2.63–4), uneasily recalling Vittoria Corombona in *The White Devil*, who 'Must personate masculine virtue'.[60] Elsewhere in Ford, most notably in *The Broken Heart*, it is sometimes the case that all characters have names of clearly symbolic or metaphoric importance; in this play, that is confined almost entirely to the female characters. Women, it seems, must be the bearers of meaning in this play rather than the makers of it, a role which is reserved for the men who construe them.

Our view of Spinella is further complicated by the obvious contrast with the more straightforward Castanna, whose name so firmly associates her with chastity. The first mention of Spinella's sister is Auria's reference to 'the comfort / Of my Spinella's sister, fair Castanna' (1.1.60–1). Almost immediately afterwards, he says to her, 'Gentle Castanna, thou art a branch of goodness' (1.1.66). It is remarkable that in a play where both Spinella and Levidolce are so easily assumed to be guilty of unchastity and Amoretta is the victim of a plot deliberately designed to humble her, no one ever has a bad word to say about Castanna. Like her sister, she is a jewel, but an unquestionably precious one: Auria cries,

> But look, Castanna's here! Welcome, fair figure
> Of a choice jewel, locked up in a cabinet,
> More precious than the public view should sully.
>
> (3.3.161–3)

Even Aurelio cannot find fault with her:

> *Auria.*   Is't not, friend,
>   An excellent maid?
> *Aurelio.*   Deserves the best of fortunes;
>   I ever spoke her virtuous.
>
> (3.3.182–4)

If Castanna is in effect a perfect character, it is particularly interesting that at the close of the play Auria chooses as her husband not his loudly righteous friend Aurelio but the notably less virtuous Adurni. This suggests that, here as in his other plays, Ford's moral vision is a complex, uneasy and not wholly conventional one, which is prepared to find merit in unexpected places and, conversely, to find conventional respectability wanting.

Auria's decision is surely an indictment of Aurelio as well as an act of building bridges with Adurni and nipping in the bud any prospective feud between them. Glenn Hopp reads Aurelio as a social climber and points out that

> In I.iii, after we have already seen Adurni's indifference to his former lover Levidolche and his new interest in Spinella, Aurelio nevertheless puffs the tainted Adurni to Futelli and Malfato. The effect, when paired with his later hasty attempts to mitigate Malfato's rage over the letter . . . is that of a flatterer who is merely out to better himself – a more noble version of Piero and Futelli.[61]

Spinella also takes an understandably uncharitable view of Aurelio's actions:

> Whiles you, belike,
> Are furnished with some news for entertainment
> Which must become your friendship, to be knit
> More fast betwixt your souls by my removal
> Both from his heart and memory.
>
> (2.4.64–8)

However, Aurelio himself attributes his motive to 'curiosity': 'You will pardon / A rash and over-busy curiosity' (5.2.176–7). This is a loaded and much-used word in Ford (see for instance *The Broken Heart* 3.1.55–6, 'Curiosity / May lead his actions into rare attempts'; 4.1.1, 'curiosity / Is of too subtle and too searching nature' and 2.1.96, 'A curiosity of admiration'), which recurs again in *The Lady's Trial* when Adurni assumes that 'report of my attempt' will have reached Auria because of 'a curiosity in youth' (4.3.12,13), which I take to mean a tendency to scrutinise closely the actions of the young, who are not yet likely to have learned discretion (though by the same token it could also suggest that the young are particularly likely to peer into things which might be better left undisturbed). The meaning that seems cumulatively to emerge from these uses is of an almost pathologically close investigation into something, perhaps the kind of introspection most closely associated with Hamlet, and certainly it is difficult to see Malvolio's curiosity as anything but officious and pernicious.

When Charles Lamb reprinted the play in his *Specimens of English Dramatic Poets* (London, 1808), he called it *The Ladies' Trial* rather than *The Lady's Trial*. As in Ford's other late play *The Fancies Chaste and Noble*, the main plot is indeed so thin and delicate that the presence of at least one sub-plot becomes virtually essential: as

Dorothy M. Farr observes, 'The main plot is the skeleton of a very
good play, but as it is, the lack of sufficient material for five acts has
to be compensated in the sub-plots'.[62] M. Joan Sargeaunt summarily
dismisses both the subplots of *The Lady's Trial*: 'Besides the main
plot, it contains two underplots; neither of these is successful.'[63]
Glenn Hopp is kinder, suggesting that 'Critics often claim that the
comic actions in Ford's plays are among the weaker elements, an
accurate comment in that Ford's farce often tends to overwork one
joke. Yet the comic plot in *The Lady's Trial* offers some of Ford's
most zestful and pleasing verbal touches'. Hopp says of Futelli and
Piero that 'Ford makes good use of these two characters . . . Because
they have connections with Adurni and Auria as well as with Guzman
and Fulgoso, Ford is able to use them at the end of II.i to make a
smooth transition from the comic plot to the main plot in prepara-
tion for Adurni's attempted seduction of Spinella.'[64] Similarly
Florence Ali observes that 'Both subplots emphasise that at all levels
of society there are strong feelings about status' and compares Futelli
and Piero to 'the doctor figures of the strongly Burtonian-influenced
plays'.[65] There seems too to be a linking element in the shape of a
parallel between the curiosity which drives Aurelio in the main plot
and the way in which the word 'imagination' echoes ominously
through Act 2, scene 1 of the play as Guzman imagines the clothes
in which he would woo Amoretta, with Futelli's reference to 'this
rich suit of imagination' (2.1.58) taking on something of a suggestion
of the emperor's new clothes. Particularly suggestive is Futelli's
assurance that 'I do [see it], as plainly as you saw the death / Of the
Austrian boar' (2.1.75–6). Futelli's words should alert us to the
importance of imagination in the main plot, but they should also
commend to our attention the characters in the subplots.

Fulgoso and Guzman serve as signposts to two principal issues.
First they, together with Benazzi, keep the question of war in the
foreground throughout the play, and second they raise the question
of ancestry. Fulgoso's supposed descent from Pantagruel is under-
lined by Malfato's musings on the question of ancestry. Malfato says
defiantly

> I read no difference between this huge,
> This monstrous big word lord, and gentleman,
> More than the title sounds; for aught I learn,
> The latter is as noble as the first;
> I'm sure more ancient.

(1.3.52–6)

Shortly afterwards, however, he backtracks significantly:

> What have I
> Deserved to be so used? In colder blood
> I do confess nobility requires
> Duty and love; it is a badge of virtue,
> By action first acquired, and next in rank
> Unto anointed royalty.

(1.3.73–8)

This play, unlike most of Ford's, is dedicated to people who are not noble (though *Love's Sacrifice* and *The Lover's Melancholy* share this characteristic, the former being dedicated to the dramatist's cousin John Ford and the latter to a group of friends including the same cousin). Perhaps, as the strains of Charles I's personal rule became ever more apparent, this is part of a general scepticism about the role of birth as a sole qualification for the wielding of power, and certainly one early owner of the play seems to have been especially struck by Malfato's defence of the gentry: the Cambridge University library copy has the words 'Icarus Icarias nomine fecit aquis' (Icarus gave his name to the Icarian Sea), from Ovid's *Tristia*, scrawled in the margin next to the Epilogue, followed by a rather garbled but fully recognisable version of 1.3.52–7.

Malfato, who helps to raise the issue of the importance of descent, is an interesting character in his own right. He is not only unlucky, as his name suggests, but also (a much more serious crime in Ford's scheme of things) insensitive. When he first presses his attentions on Spinella, she delicately affects not to understand him:

> An understanding dulled by th'infelicity
> Of constant sorrow is not apprehensive
> In pregnant novelty; my ears receive
> The words you utter, cousin, but my thoughts
> Are fastened on another subject.

(4.1.57–61)

Delicacy, however, is wasted on Malfato. Even when Spinella openly reproves him, it is unclear whether or not he actually falls silent:

> *Spinella.* No more; I dare not hear it.
> *Malfato.*   All is said:
>   Henceforth shall never syllable proceed
>   From my unpleasant voice of amorous folly –

(4.1.77–9)

Gifford put a full stop at the end of this speech of Malfato's, and
in one of his rare comments observes that 'Malfato has hitherto
appeared to little advantage; but the author makes him full amends
in this beautiful scene'. Q, however, has a long dash, suggesting that
Malfato is interrupted by the arrival of Castanna, and that, had he
not been, he might in fact have said more despite his protestations
that he was not about to do so, and I have retained that punctuation,
with its suggestion that Malfato is interrupted rather than that he
does indeed keep his promise to stop speaking voluntarily. Malfato
is also slow to understand what other people think and feel. First,
Castanna tells Spinella of Auria's faith in her:

> *Castanna.* Methinks the news should cause some motion, sister.
>   You are not well.
> *Malfato.*   Not well?
> *Spinella.*   I am unworthy.
> *Malfato.* Of whom? What? Why?
> *Spinella.*   Go, cousin; come, Castanna.
>
> (4.1.114–16)

Second, Auria arranges a marriage between Castanna and Adurni:

> *Auria.*   Yours, to whose faith
>   I am a guardian, not by imposition,
>   But by you chosen. Look ye, I have fitted
>   A husband for you, noble and deserving;
>   No shrinking back. – Adurni, I present her,
>   A wife of worth.
> *Malfato.*   How's that?
>
> (5.2.146–51)

Again, Malfato is entirely wrongfooted.

Malfato's obtuseness serves to reveal the extent to which what the
characters do not say in this play is almost as important as what
they do say. In this it resembles *The Fancies Chaste and Noble*, which
has a similar aesthetic of silence. In *The Fancies*, Flavia, who declares
herself one of 'those wives whose innocence / Stranger to language,
spoke obedience only' (2.1.104–5), says to her brother,

>   let us meete
> And talke a little, we perhaps may chide
> At first, shed some few teares, and then be quiet;
> There's all.
>
> (3.2.137–40)

The same phenomenon can be observed in *The Broken Heart*, where Penthea 'is left a prey to words' (4.2.45), and Prophilus says of Ithocles that

> Sadness grows
> Upon his recreations, which he hoards
> In such a willing silence, that to question
> The grounds will argue little skill in friendship
> And less good manners.

(2.3.6–10)

In *The Lady's Trial*, Auria says to Aurelio 'Friends we are, and will embrace; but let's not speak / Another word' (1.1.220–1). Robert Davril suggested that 'When he became aware of the possibilities of silence on the stage, Ford made it one of the basic elements of his dramatic technique and psychology. It is not exaggerated to say that all his women, to some degree, are like Calantha and Cordelia, and owe much of their dignity and nobleness to their restraint and to their silent attitude',[66] and Havelock Ellis well observed of Ford that

> It is the grief deeper than language that he strives to express . . . He is a master of the brief mysterious words, so calm in seeming, which well up from the depths of despair. He concentrates the revelation of a soul's agony into a sob or a sigh. The surface seems calm; we scarcely suspect that there is anything beneath; one gasp bubbles up from the drowning heart below, and all is silence.[67]

Glenn Hopp writes that 'In language and tone *The Lady's Trial* stands at the opposite end of the Ford canon from *'Tis Pity She's a Whore* . . . This play is closer in feeling to the hushed tones of *The Broken Heart* than to the louder vengeance of *'Tis Pity*'.[68]

An aesthetic of silence, though, is not one that sits easily on the stage. Eugene M. Waith calls *The Lady's Trial* 'the least spectacular of all the plays',[69] and Glenn Hopp suggests that the play 'may perhaps be best appreciated as a closet drama or as an interesting experiment that yielded mixed results toward the end of his career'.[70] Perhaps this might in any case have been Ford's last play – he was ageing, and, when Christopher Beeston, manager of the Cockpit and father-in-law of his friend Theophilus Bird, died in October 1638, he might well have felt that he had lost a vital element of what made his drama possible – but it is impossible not to observe that he has, in a sense, quite simply written himself into silence.

There are twenty-nine surviving copies of the 1639 quarto. Nogami offers a very detailed account of the text (pp. 106–22) and argues for two compositors, of whom the more accurate was responsible for B through to H and K (pp. 109–10). He also notes that the catchword on F2r appears as 'Ey' on the Morgan copy, which is also missing A3, and 'By' on all others, perhaps suggesting a stop-press correction (p. 107). The same explanation presumably also accounts for the fact that the prologue is unsigned in the copy in Boston, the second Folger copy, and also Longe, Morgan, and Wrenn 1 (in which A3 and A4 are also reversed), so that it was apparently added after the run had started. The second Dyce copy lacks the stage direction '*Enter* AURIA and AURELIO' at 5.2.12. This also offers the first instance of an apparent disordering of the type in the word 'fortunes' at 5.2.33, which apparently persists for the remainder of the run. Apart from the dedication, the play entirely lacks Ford's characteristic lavish use of italics for emphasis, on which many critics have commented.[71] It therefore looks as though the copy may have originated in the theatre rather than from Ford's own papers, with the dedication being added later.

Many copies are not well printed and several show damaged type and ink blotching. The second Folger copy has badly chewed margins, which may perhaps be why one early reader found his attention wandering so much that underneath the epilogue he wrote 'To Mrs Ann Chichester / I Love Dearly' followed by an undecipherable monogram. Other copies also have handwritten annotations, some of which do not bespeak a very great deal of attention to the play: the King's College, Cambridge, copy has the handwritten annotation 'by John Ford. a Tragedy' on the title page directly underneath the title, while in the Chicago copy, which is very badly ink-blotched at the start of Act 2 and intermittently thereafter, someone (perhaps in 1795 when, according to the frontispiece, the copy was collated and found to be perfect, or perhaps in 1901, the date at the end), has written on the blank page opposite the end of the dedication to the Wyrleys 'It will be difficult to find John Forde's equal in the pompous insipidity and laboured nothingness of his Dedications'. However, one of the three copies at the University of Texas has been copiously larded with crosses in the margin, and bears in what looks like a nineteenth-century hand the repeated phrase 'Bouna' or 'Muy bouna' (presumably 'bueno', so 'good' and 'very good'), and the more substantial comments 'This whole scene very good' next to 3.3.93–100, where Auria confronts Aurelio about his suspicions of Spinella, and 'A very good scene' next to 4.3.1–3, where Auria and Aurelio receive Adurni. One oddity which all surviving copies have in common is a misnumbering of the signatures: the dedication appears on sig. A3r; Act 1 begins on sig. B1r; the next sheet is marked A3 again and the next after that is marked B3.

Nogami, as we have seen, regards one compositor as more error-prone than the other, and Joe Andrew Sutfin comments that 'There is a marked deterioration in the quality of the printing in the last four sheets, perhaps due to the difficulty of the matter being set',[72] that is Amoretta's lisp and Fulgoso and Guzman's foreign words. However, the text of The Lady's Trial is generally fairly clean except for the vexed question of whether Benazzi is speaking verse or prose. Q is not always careful to make this distinction in any case, and can indeed be careless about lineation in general, and there are several instances where either choice would be possible. At a number of points (e.g. 3.4.29–36), I have chosen to follow the apparent warrant of Q and have Benazzi speak verse, despite the fact that Weber, Gifford, Keltie, and Nogami do not, because I see Benazzi's gradual move to verse as linked to his gradual reintegration into society. Conversely at 5.1.22–3 Benazzi's speech is laid out as two lines of verse in Q, but its nineteen syllables do not conform to iambic beat, and both his other speeches in this scene are in prose, something which presumably confirms him as an outsider to the verse-speaking Martino.

The first edition of the play was Weber's, in 1811. As the play's next editor, William Gifford, was quick to point out, Weber was careless, missing many obvious emendations such as the obviously necessary change to 'serenity' at 4.3.10, and printing 'womens' at 5.2.108. He omitted the whole of 2.1.179 and cheerfully printed the clearly nonsensical 'Skirmish of words hath with your wife lewdly ranged' (5.2.115). He did, however, have a good ear for an iambic line, and even Gifford, who poured scorn on him, silently followed his 'He'll' rather than 'He' at 4.2.153. Gifford's own, much more careful edition was essentially followed by John Keltie in his The Works of the British Dramatists (Edinburgh, 1870), which represents Ford by The Lady's Trial alone, with the comment 'after much consideration we have deemed The Lady's Trial most suitable for insertion in these pages',[73] presumably because it was free of incest, adultery, or violence. The volume also features Lyly (Alexander and

Campaspe), Peele (*David and Bethsabe*), Greene (*Friar Bacon and Friar Bungay*), Marlowe (*Edward II* and *Doctor Faustus*), Jonson (*The Alchemist, Epicoene, Every Man In*), Beaumont and Fletcher (*Philaster, A King and No King* and *The Knight of the Burning Pestle*), Webster (*The Duchess of Malfi*), Marston (the two Antonio plays), Masssinger (*The Virgin Martyr, The Duke of Milan*, and *A New Way to Pay Old Debts*), Heywood (*A Woman Killed with Kindness*) and Shirley (*The Traitor* and *The Brothers*). Keltie largely relies on Gifford's text (though with an occasional preference for Weber's, as at 4.1.82 where he prefers Weber's 'wi'you' to Gifford's 'w'ye'); he does, however, often cite Weber's notes verbatim, but none of Gifford's.

In the late twentieth century, the play was edited by Katsuhiko Nogami for a PhD at the Shakespeare Institute. The copy of this thesis which Dr Nogami very kindly gave me marks some corrections in pencil which do not appear in the final bound copy of the thesis, so I list these (and a few others) in the accompanying note.[74]

The copy-text for this edition is the copy in the Henry E. Huntington Library, Sam Marino, California, available on Early English Books Online.

STAGE HISTORY

The Lady's Trial announces on its title page that it was 'Acted by both their Majesties' Servants at the private house in Drury Lane'. This company, more usually referred to as 'Beeston's boys', played at the Phoenix Theatre in Drury Lane, also known as the Cockpit, which was managed by Christopher Beeston. Joe Andrew Sutfin notes that *The Lady's Trial* was not listed amongst the plays which Beeston sought to have protected by the Lord Chamberlain the next year and hence infers that it was not a great success,[75] but we have no solid information about this first prodution.

Ford seems, however, to have been considered stageworthy well into the seventeenth century. *'Tis Pity She's a Whore* was performed in 1661 and again for several months in 1663,[76] and *Love's Sacrifice* c. 1663–64. R. F. Hill notes that

> *The Lover's Melancholy* and *The Broken Heart* were on a list of plays assigned to Davenant and the Duke's Company, 20 August 1668, but there is no record of Restoration performances ... One of the Folger Shakespeare Library copies (11163, copy 3) of *The Lover's Melancholy* was at some time being prepared for a production, although there are no signs that it was ever actually used in the theatre.

Hill further observes that 'Clifford Leech has detailed and analysed the cuts and markings; such evidence as these afford points to a seventeenth-century, post-Restoration, dating'.[77]

In the case of *The Lady's Trial*, the Columbia University library copy of the quarto has been annotated for one or more performances or productions during the Restoration period, perhaps that which Pepys saw on 3 March 1669, when he noted that he took his wife 'to the Duke of York's playhouse and there saw an old play, the first time acted these 40 years, called *The Lady's tryall*, acted only by the young people of the House, but the House very full. But it is but a sorry play'.[78]

The signatures of this copy have been supplemented with hand-written Arabic numerals at the top left- and right-hand corners and the initial cast list has been annotated with a number of names of performers, headed by that of Thomas Betterton, which appears just above 'Auria, a noble Genoese'. To the right of that appears the name 'Moon', i.e. Michael Mohun (c. 1616–84). This name is a particularly interesting one because, although nothing can be securely established about his background, it is perhaps not impossible that he was related to the Mohun family to a member of which *The Queen* was dedicated. From 1636 Mohun was a member of Beeston's company, so he may well have acted in the original production of *The Lady's Trial*, and he married the daughter of Theophilus Bird, who signed the prologue of *The Lady's Trial*. Although apparently of small stature, Mohun was much famed for his acting and after the Restoration he became famous for, amongst other roles, Face in *The Alchemist* and Iago in *Othello*. As for why both his name and Betterton's seem to be attached to the character of Auria, Pepys noted that Betterton was ill and unable to act from at least 16 October 1667 to mid-1668, so it may be that Mohun took the role during that period, or it may be that there were essentially two separate productions, for next to the name of Adurni is a Greek delta followed by 'Harris: hart', i.e. Henry Harris and Charles Hart; Aurelio is followed first by a name which may be Solomon and then, slightly above that, that of Byrd, i.e. Theophilus Bird, who signed the Prologue; and Malfato has 'Morice' scribbled to the left but what looks like 'Kaniston' – i.e. Edward Kynaston, whose other known roles included Roseilli and Caraffa in *Love's Sacrifice* – to the right. Other roles have only one name associated with them – Trelcatio is assigned to Burt, Martino to 'Blagdun', Piero to 'Shatterel' and Fulgoso to 'hart – but other handwritten names, not always compatible with this list, appear above the names of some characters on their first entrance. At 1.1. the name of 'R. Nake' (?) appears above 'Piero' and 'Sandford' above Futilli. When Adurni and Auria makes their first entrance 'Cadymus? Smith?' appears above the name of Adurni, while above that of Auria is simply 'Smith', presumably William Smith who took over several of Harris's roles. Aurelio's name when he first appears has 'Mohhun' (?) above, and Martino's 'Hartford'. *The Lady's Trial* seems, then, to have been popular for at least a short time after the Restoration, but I know of no productions since.

NOTES

1 The traditional date of 17 April 1586 has recently been corrected by Antony Telford Moore ('The date of John Ford's baptism', *N&Q* 41.1 (March 1994): 70–1). For the author's life and works, see also the very full account offered by Derek Roper in his Revels edition of *'Tis Pity She's a Whore* (Manchester: Manchester University Press, 1975), pp. xix–xxvi. My own account builds on his but takes note of work published in the intervening years.
2 See R. G. Howarth, 'John Webster, property-owner?', *N&Q* n.s. 12.6 (1965): 236–7.
3 See R. G. Howarth, 'John Ford', *N&Q* 202 (June 1957): 240.
4 See Brian Vickers, *Counterfeiting Shakespeare: Evidence, Authorship, and John Ford's Funerall Elegye* (Cambridge: Cambridge University Press), 2002.
5 See Lisa Hopkins, 'Lillo's *The London Merchant*: an Elizabethan palimpsest?', *English Language Notes* 36:2 (December, 1998): 4–11.
6 Alfred Harbage, 'Elizabethan-Restoration palimpsest', *Modern Language Review* 35 (1940): 287–319, p. 300.
7 G. F. Sensabaugh, 'Another play by John Ford', *Modern Language Quarterly* 3 (1942): 595–601, p. 595.
8 Robert Davril, *Le Drame de John Ford* (Paris: Librairie Marcel Didier, 1954), p. 317.
9 H. J. Oliver, *The Problem of John Ford* (Melbourne: Melbourne University Press, 1955), p. 135.
10 M. E. Shewring, '*The Great Favourite*; or, *The Duke of Lerma*, attributed to Sir Robert Howard', PhD diss., University of Birmingham, 1977, introduction, p. 14.
11 Lesel Dawson, 'Dangerous misogyny: John Ford's *The Queen* and the Earl of Essex's 1601 uprising', *Explorations in Renaissance Culture* 33.1 (2007): 64–82.
12 Nogami, introduction, pp. 100–1.
13 F. G. Fleay, *A Biographical Chronicle of the English Drama* (London: Reeves and Turner, 1891), 2 vols, 1, p. 234.
14 Joe Andrew Sutfin, 'Ford's *Love's Sacrifice*, *The Lady's Trial*, and *The Queen*, critical old spelling editions of the texts of the original quartos', PhD diss., Vanderbilt University, 1964, p. 154.

15 Sir Walter Ralegh, *The Discoverie of the Large, Rich and Bewtiful Empyre of Guiana*, ed. Neil L. Whitehead (Manchester: Manchester University Press, 1997), pp. 136, 149 and 194. Katsuhiko Nogami in his edition of the play also dismisses Sutfin's suggestion (introduction, p. 4).

16 See for instance Matheo Aleman, *The Rogue, or the Life of Guzman de Alfarache*, trans. James Mabbe, ed. James Fitzmaurice-Kelly (London: Constable, 1924), 4 vols, 2, pp. 78–9.

17 *The Rogue*..., 1, p. 25.

18 See my forthcoming edition of *The Broken Heart* in *The Complete Works of John Ford* (Oxford: Oxford University Press, forthcoming).

19 *The Rogue*..., 4, p. 6.

20 Nogami, 10 and 8.

21 Nogami, 82 and 94.

22 Jonson, *The Alchemist*, 3.3.18–19.

23 See Javier de Santiago Fernández and José María de Francisco Olmos, 'La Inscripción de la fachada del palacio del Infantado en Guadalajara', *Documenta & Instrumenta* 4 (2006): 131–50, p. 146.

24 Thomas Scott's *SirWalter Raleighs Ghost, or Englands forewarner Discouering a secret consultation, newly holden in the Court of Spaine* (Utrecht, 1626), pp. 2 and 17.

25 Richard Jones, *The Booke of Honor and Armes*, London, 1590, Book Four, p. 50, Book Five, p. 16, and Book Five, p. 28.

26 Anthony Copley, *Wits, Fittes and Fancies Fronted and entermedled with presidentes of honour and wisdome* (London, 1595), pp. 13, 129, 16, 18, 62 and 24.

27 Leanda de Lisle, *After Elizabeth* (London: Harper Collins, 2006), p. 248.

28 Mark Nicholls, 'Treason's reward: the punishment of conspirators in the Bye Plot of 1603', *The Historical Journal* 38.4 (December 1995): 821–42, p. 823.

29 Nicholls, 'Treason's reward', p. 834.

30 Andrew Boyle, 'Hans Eworth's portrait of the Earl of Arundel and the politics of 1549–50', *English Historical Review* 117 [470] (February 2002): 25–47, p. 38.

31 *Ibid.*, p. 45.

32 Catherine Grace Canino, *Shakespeare and the Nobility* (Cambridge: Cambridge University Press, 2007), p. 7.

33 Sir H. C. Maxwell Lyte, *A History of Dunster and of the Families of Mohun and Luttrell*, 2 vols (London: the St Catherine Press Ltd, 1909), 1, p. 165, and 2, p. 511.

34 *Ibid.*, p. 50.

35 *The Rogue*, 2, p. 178.

36 John Marston, *The Malcontent*, ed. G. K. Hunter (Manchester: Manchester University Press, 1975), 3.2.28–9.

37 Charles Hughes, *Shakespeare's Europe: Unpublished Chapters of Fynes Moryson's Itinerary* (London: Sherratt & Hughes, 1903), pp. 110–11, 114 and 100–1.

38 John Ford, *The Golden Meane*, in *The Nondramatic Works of John Ford*, ed. L. E. Stock, Gilles D. Monsarrat, Judith M. Kennedy and Dennis

Danielson (Binghamton, NY: Medieval and Renaissance Texts & Studies,
1991), pp. 248 and 268.
39 John Ford, *Christes Bloodie Sweat*, in *The Nondramatic Works*, p. 171.
40 John Ford, *Linea Vitae: A Line of Life*, in *The Nondramatic Works*, p. 303.
41 'Shorter pieces', in *The Nondramatic Works*, p. 355.
42 Charles Saltonstall, *The Navigator* (London: printed for George Herlock,
1636), pp. 5 and 13.
43 See Ralph A. Griffiths, *Sir Rhys ap Thomas and His Family* (Cardiff:
University of Wales Press, 1993), p. 130.
44 Charles Nicholl, *The Creature in the Map* [1995] (London: Vintage, 1996),
pp. 60 and 274–5.
45 Samuel Bawlf, *The Secret Voyage of Sir Francis Drake* (Harmondsworth:
Penguin, 2003), pp. 251 and 253.
46 Lois E. Bueler, 'Role-splitting and reintegration: the tested woman plot
in Ford', *Studies in English Literature* 20.2 (Spring 1980): 325–44, p. 325.
47 Brian Opie, '"Being all one": Ford's analysis of love and friendship in
Loues Sacrifice and *The Ladies Triall*', in *John Ford: Critical Re-Visions*,
ed. Michael Neill (Cambridge: Cambridge University Press), 1988,
pp. 233–60.
48 Dorothy M. Farr, *John Ford and the Caroline Theatre* (Basingstoke:
Palgrave Macmillan, 1979), p. 125.
49 J. Ford, *Fames Memoriall*, in *The Nondramatic Works*, p. 104.
50 Verna Foster, ' *'Tis Pity She's a Whore* as city tragedy', in *John Ford: Critical
Revisions*, ed. Michael Neill (Cambridge: Cambridge University Press,
1988), pp. 181–200.
51 Subha Mukherji, 'False trials in Shakespeare, Massinger, and Ford',
Essays in Criticism 56.3 (July 2006): 219–40, pp. 222 and 231.
52 James Howe, 'Ford's *The Lady's Trial*: a play of metaphysical wit', *Genre*
7.4 (1974): 342–61, pp. 342–3.
53 *Ibid.*, p. 342.
54 Mukherji, 'False trials in Shakespeare, Massinger, and Ford', p. 225.
55 On the prevalence of lawyers in London theatre audiences, see for
instance Philip J. Finkelpearl, *John Marston of the Middle Temple*
(Cambridge, MA.: Harvard University Press, 1969), p. 27, and Francis
Beaumont and John Fletcher, *Philaster*, ed. Andrew Gurr (London:
Methuen, 1969), introduction, p. xiii.
56 J. Ford, *Fames Memoriall*, p. 130.
57 J. Ford, *Love's Sacrifice*, edited by A. T. Moore (Manchester: Manchester
University Press, 2002), 1.2.131–3.
58 Peter Martyr, *The history of trauayle in the West and Easy Indies, and other
countreys lying eyther way, towardes the fruitfull and ryche Moluccaes . . .*,
trans. Richard Eden (London, 1577), p. 424.
59 Thelma N. Greenfield, 'John Ford's tragedy: the challenge of re-
engagement', in *'Concord in Discord': The Plays of John Ford, 1586–1986*,
ed. Donald K. Anderson, Jr (New York: AMS Press, 1986), pp. 1–26,
p. 17.
60 John Webster, *The White Devil*, ed. John Russell Brown (London:
Methuen, 1960), 1.3.136.
61 Glenn Hopp, 'The speaking voice in *The Lady's Trial*', in *'Concord in
Discord': The Plays of John Ford, 1586–1986*, pp. 149–70, p. 165.

62 Farr, *John Ford and the Caroline Theatre*, p. 144.
63 Sargeaunt, 75.
64 Hopp, 'The speaking voice in *The Lady's Trial*', pp. 150 and 158.
65 Florence Ali, *Opposing Absolutes: Conviction and Convention in John Ford's Plays* (Salzburg: Institut für Englische Sprache und Literatur, 1974), pp. 80 and 82.
66 Robert Davril, 'Shakespeare and Ford', *Shakespeare Jahrbuch* 94 (1958): 121–31, p. 129.
67 *John Ford*, ed. Havelock Ellis (London: T. Fisher Unwin, n.d.), introduction, pp. xiv–xv.
68 Hopp, 'The speaking voice in *The Lady's Trial*', p. 149.
69 Eugene M. Waith, 'John Ford and the final exultation of love', in *'Concord in Discord': The Plays of John Ford, 1586–1986*, ed. Donald K. Anderson, Jr (New York: AMS Press, 1986), pp. 49–60, p. 58.
70 Hopp, 'The speaking voice in *The Lady's Trial*', p. 150.
71 See for instance R. J. Fehrenbach, 'Typographical variation in ford's texts: accidentals or substantives', in *'Concord in Discord': The Plays of John Ford, 1586–1986*, ed. Donald K. Anderson, Jr (New York: AMS Press, 1986), pp. 265–94.
72 Sutfin, 'Ford's *Love's Sacrifice*, *The Lady's Trial*, and *The Queen*', p. 155.
73 Keltie, p. 461.
74 1.3.44 *Sure* for *Secure*; 2.1.102 *advance* for *adventure*; 2.1.126 *an't* for *and*; 2.1. 202 *variant* for *valiant*; 2.2.63 *ay* for *I*; 2.2.70 *Damn up* for *Dam up*; 2.4.90 *for* omitted; 3.2.30 *await* for *wait*; 3.2.52 *I am* for *I'm*; 4.1.58 *Of* omitted; 4.2.139 *Piccaro* for *Picaro*; 4.2.172 *My* for *Mine*; 4.3.70 *on th'other* for *on the her*; 4.3.123 *take* for *talk*; 5.1.24 *poor* for *proper*; 5.1.29 *sister's* for *niece's*; 5.1.48 *resolve* for *resolute*.
75 Sutfin, 'Ford's *Love's Sacrifice*, *The Lady's Trial*, and *The Queen*', p. 153.
76 John Ford, *'Tis Pity She's a Whore*, ed. Roper, introduction, p. lvii.
77 John Ford, *The Lover's Melancholy*, ed. R. F. Hill (Manchester: Manchester University Press, 1985), introduction, p. 33.
78 Samuel Pepys, *The Diary*, ed. R. C. Latham and W. Matthews, 11 vols (London, 1970–83), 9, p. 465. Though this does not seem to have stopped him from buying the play, because the first Folger library copy of the quarto bears Pepys's motto, 'Mens cujusque is est quisque', and was annotated by Henry B. Wheatley as 'Bibliotheca Pepysiana secund HBW 1904, Walker & Cockerell Ph. Sc.'.

THE LADY'S TRIAL

THE LADY'S TRIAL

Acted
by both their Majesties' Servants
at the private house in
Drury Lane.

FIDE HONOR

London.
Printed by E. G. for Henry Shephard, and are to be
sold in his shop in Chancery Lane at the sign of
the Bible, between Sargeants Inn and Fleet Street,
near the King's Head Tavern. 1639.

---

3. *both their Majesties' servants*] This company, more usually referred to as 'Beeston's Boys', was referred to by William Beeston in his will, drawn up on 4 October 1638, as 'the company for the King's and Queen's service' (*EPT* 633-4), and is also sometimes called the King and Queen's Young Company. See Gurr 423-4 for a description of their personnel.

4-5. *the private house in Drury Lane*] The Phoenix Theatre, also known as the Cockpit, being managed by Christopher Beeston after the death of his father William.

6. *FIDE HONOR*] 'Fide honor', an anagram of 'Iohn Forde', first appears on the title page of *The Broken Heart* (1633), and thereafter on all Ford's plays published during the 1630s, *Perkin Warbeck* (1634), *The Fancies Chaste and Noble* (1638) and *The Lady's Trial* (1638). Its literal meaning of 'honour by faith' might allude either to personal integrity or perhaps to religious faith.

8. *E. G.*] Probably Edward Griffin, younger of that name (Nogami 245-6).

Henry Shephard] The publisher Henry Shephard kept two shops, one of which, operating in Chancery Lane from 1636 to 1646, carried the sign of the Bible (Nogami 246).

10. *Sargeants Inn*] A building in Chancery Lane originally designed for the accommodation of sargeants-at-law and judges.

11. *King's Head Tavern*] On the north side of Fleet Street, opposite the Queen's Head.

[Epistle Dedicatory]

To my deservingly honoured John Wyrley Esquire, and to the virtuous and right worthy gentlewoman, Mistress Mary Wyrley his wife, this service.

The inequality of retribution turns to a pity when there is not ability sufficient for acknowledgement. Your equal respects may yet admit the readiness of endeavour, though the very hazard in it betray my defect. I have enjoyed freely acquaintance with the sweetness of your dispositions; and can justly 5 account, from the nobleness of them, an evident distinction betwixt friendship and friends. The latter (according to the practice of compliment) are usually met with, and often

---

8. compliment] *Weber*; complement *Q*.

0.1–3.] John (later Sir John) Wyrley (1607–87) was the son of Humphrey Wyrley of Hamstead Hall, Handsworth, near Birmingham, and his wife Knightley Wyrley. In common with other prominent local families, the Wyrleys were Catholic. John Wyrley matriculated at Magdalen Hall, Oxford, on 17 May 1622 and entered Gray's Inn on 27 May 1625. His wife Mary was the daughter of Sir Francis Wolley, friend of John Donne and cousin of his wife Anne More; Sir Francis Wolley gave shelter to the Donnes when their marriage displeased Anne's father, and Ford's friendship with the Donnes' son George, who wrote commendatory verses for *The Lover's Melancholy*, may have provided his link to the Wyrleys, or it could have arisen through John Wyrley's attendance at Gray's Inn, of which the author's cousin John Ford, dedicatee of *Love's Sacrifice*, was a member, as was Robert Ellice, a co-dedicatee of *The Lover's Melancholy*. Indeed Robert Ellice and John Wyrley had matriculated at Magdalen within a few months of each other, on 31 January 1622/3 and 17 May 1622 respectively, and this made them close contemporaries of William, Lord Craven, recipient of the dedication of *The Broken Heart* in 1633. The second volume of Fuller's *The Church History of Britain* was also dedicated to John Wyrley. A staunch royalist, John Wyrley was knighted by Charles I at Whitehall in 1641. John and Mary Wyrley were childless and on his death in 1687 John Wyrley was succeeded by his nephew Humphrey Wyrley.
    8. *compliment*] For this usage (and for the contemporary concurrence with Ford's preferred spelling of 'complement'), see *OED* 9, 'A ceremonious or formal tribute of (mere) courtesy paid to anyone'.

without search. The other many have searched for, I have
found, for which, though I partake a benefit of the fortune,   10
yet to you, most equal pair, must remain the honour of that
bounty. In presenting this issue of some less serious hours to
your tuition, I appeal from the severity of censure to the mercy
of your judgements; and shall rate it at a higher value than
when it was mine own, if you only allow it the favour of adop-   15
tion. Thus, as your happiness in the fruition of each other's
love proceeds to a constancy, so the truth of mine shall appear
less unshaken, as you shall please to continue in your good
opinions.

                                                    JOHN FORD

9–12.] Ford seems to be saying something like 'many have sought for
friendship; I have actually found it, but all the merit of that belongs entirely
to the two of you – I am merely the lucky recipient'.

12–14.] The reference to 'this issue' inaugurates a series of birth and
childrearing metaphors – 'adoption' and 'fruition' – which collectively figure
the play as a child which its father, Ford, is offering to the benevolent foster-
age of the Wyrleys. The date of the Wyrleys' marriage is not recorded, but it
was perhaps already apparent that it would remain childless; if so, the play
is perhaps being offered as a substitute for the offspring which did not arrive.

15–16. *if . . . adoption*] This is poised delicately between resembling the
modern meaning of 'if only' and complimenting the Wyrleys on the unique
properties of adoption by them.

18. *less unshaken*] Nogami compares to 'less unattempted' at 4.3.68, but
the meaning there seems in fact to be '(un)'less unattempted', which would
not make sense here. Ford seems rather to be saying that the longer the
Wyrleys continue to think well of him and his play, the more firmly established his own rather tentative (i.e. potentially to be shaken) happiness will
become.

The Speakers

AURIA, a noble Genoese.
ADURNI, a young lord.
AURELIO, friend to Auria.
MALFATO, a discontented lover, cousin of Spinella and
    Castanna.   5
TRELCATIO, a citizen of Genoa and uncle of Auria.
MARTINO, a citizen of Genoa, great-uncle of Levidolce.
PIERO, a dependant on Adurni.
FUTELLI, a dependant on Adurni.
GUZMAN, a braggadocio Spaniard.   10
FULGOSO, an upstart gallant.
BENAZZI, husband to Levidolce.
SPINELLA, wife to Auria.

6–7. a citizen of . . .] *This ed.; in Q, the names of Trelcatio and Martino are
linked by a brace followed by 'Citizens of Genoa'.*   8–9. a dependant on] *This
ed.; in Q, the names of Trelcatio and Martino are linked by a brace followed by
'Dependants on Adurni'.*

---

1. *AURIA*] Doria was the name of one of the most important families in
Genoa, whose most distinguished scion was Andrea Doria, who fought at
the battle of Lepanto. In Fynes Moryson's *Itinerary* the name is spelt D'Auria,
which is presumably what lies behind Ford's Auria.

2. *ADURNI*] The choice of name was possibly influenced by the fact that
the husband of St Catherine of Genoa was Giuliano Adorno. Ford would
have found in Moryson and in Burton's *The Anatomy of Melancholy*, on which
he drew extensively in other plays, the mention of the Adurni as a prominent
Genoese family.

4. *MALFATO*] Literally 'ill-fated one'.

10. *GUZMAN*] The name of the rogue in Mateo Alemán's *The Rogue: or
the life of Guzman de Alfarache*, translated into English by James Mabbe and
printed in 1622.

11. *FULGOSO*] The name of a giant in Diego Ortúñez de Calahorra's *The
second part of the first booke of the Mirrour of Knighthoode*, translated into
English in 1599. Frederick Fulgoso is also mentioned in Ariosto's *Orlando
Furioso*, translated into English by Sir John Harington.

13. *SPINELLA*] Presumably derives from spinel, a precious stone which is
red in colour and resembles a ruby. Ford was interested in jewels, referring
to amethysts in *The Broken Heart* (4.2.130) and including in *The Fancies
Chaste and Noble* a discussion about whether or not a gentleman should have
some skill as a lapidary (5.3.43–50).

CASTANNA, her sister.
AMORETTA, a fantastic maid.   15
LEVIDOLCE, a wanton.

The Scene: GENOA

---

14. *CASTANNA*] In a marginal note in the third chapter of the first book of Mateo Alemán's *The Rogue: or the life of Guzman de Alfarache*, the name Castanna is glossed as 'chestnut'. Like Castamela in Ford's own *The Fancies Chaste and Noble*, Castiza in Middleton's *The Revenger's Tragedy* and Castabella in Tourneur's *The Atheist's Tragedy*, Castanna's role in the play is indicated by the fact that the first part of her name is derived from the Latin 'casta', chaste.

15. *fantastic*] motivated by fancy and fantasy. The name Amoretta, literally 'little love', is also found in Spenser's *The Faerie Queene* and Middleton's *The Witch*.

16. *LEVIDOLCE*] In Italian, literally 'light and sweet'. *The Atheist's Tragedy* contains a Levidulcia whose wantonness is contrasted with the chastity of the heroine Castabella.

Prologue

Language and matter, with a fit of mirth
That sharply savours more of air than earth,
Like midwives, bring a play to timely birth.

But where's now such a one in which these three
Are handsomely contrived? Or if they be,   5
Are understood by all who hear to see?

Wit, wit's the word in fashion, that alone
Cries up the poet, which, though neatly shown,
Is rather censured oftentimes than known.

---

1. *fit*] snatch of music or stanza or of a song; John Florio's *Queen Anna's New World of Words* (London, 1611) offers the definition 'a fit of mirth or fidling' for the term 'Stampináta'. Here it may also have the metaphorical sense of something like 'merry interlude' or 'passage of wit', as in the title of Anthony Copley's *Wits, Fittes and Fancies Fronted and entermedled with presidentes of honour and wisdome* (1595), a probable source for the play (see introduction, pp. 9–11); perhaps playing on both the older meaning of part of a literary composition (though usually specifically a poem) and also on *OED* n.2, 4, 'a sudden and transitory state of activity or inaction, or of any specified kind of activity, feeling, inclination, or aptitude'.

2. *savours … earth*] Partakes of the spiritual rather than of the earthy, i.e. is not bawdy.

3. *midwives*] Drawing on a common trope in the period, this term also develops the birth imagery of the Epistle Dedicatory.

6. *all who hear to see*] Gabriel Egan has shown that though the term 'to see a play' was more common in the period than 'to hear a play', three-eighths of the instances of 'hear a play' come from Shakespeare, so the phrase may have suggested greater discernment (Egan 332). Ford seems to suggest that it is difficult now to find occasions when discriminating audiences engage properly with serious, well-written plays which are leavened with comic relief of a suitable nature.

8. *Cries up*] secures a reputation for, proclaims to be excellent.
neatly] elegantly.

9.] Is more often criticised than recognised.

He who will venture on a jest, that can   10
Rail on another's pain, or idly scan
Affairs of state, oh, he's the only man –

A goodly approbation, which must bring
Fame with contempt, by such a deadly sting;
The Muses chatter, who were wont to sing.   15

Your favours in what we present today;
Our fearless author boldly bids me say
He tenders you no satire, but a play;

In which, if so he have not hit all right,
For wit, words, mirth, and matter, as he might,   20
'A wishes yet 'a had for your delight.

                                        MR BIRD

10–15.] Ford, often laconic, here verges on obscurity. He begins by lament-
ing the approbation afforded to those whose work offers topicality by alluding
to real people's lives or public affairs; the kind of fame such approbation
brings must always be accompanied by contempt, and leads to a debased art.

15.] Poets now relay gossip instead of following epic tradition by speaking
of great events. 'Sing' alludes to the typical epic statement of purpose, such as
Virgil's 'Arma virumque cano' ('Of arms and the man I sing') which opens the
Aeneid; 'chatter' suggests much more frivolous and mundane conversation.

16.] Presumably we need to infer that a request is being made for the
'favours'; cf the similarly bald-seeming request for 'Your pardon' in *The
Broken Heart* (*BH* 1.1.96).

20. *wit, words, mirth, and matter*] Ford reverts here to the four criteria
which he earlier identified as essential to a good play.

21. *'A*] he.

22. *MR BIRD*] The actor Theophilus Bird also joined with his colleague
Andrew Penneycuicke to preface a dedication to Thomas Wriothesley, fourth
earl of Southampton, to the beginning of *The Sun's Darling*, a masque by
Ford and Dekker, when it was published in 1657, and wrote a prologue for
Ford and Dekker's *The Witch of Edmonton* in 1658 which concludes with the
words 'Here is mirth and matter'. *DNB* tentatively identifies this Theophilus
Bird with the child baptised on 7 December 1608 by William Bird or Borne,
an actor with Prince Henry's Men, who was one of two men paid by
Henslowe for additions to Marlowe's *Doctor Faustus*; Theophilus Bird was
certainly the son-in-law of Christopher Beeston, manager of the Cockpit,
and seems to have been a member of Beeston's Boys, the resident company
at the Cockpit, until some time after Beeston's death in October 1638. He
played women's parts at first, but by 1635 is known to have been taking male
roles, since the cast list for Thomas Nabbes's *Hannibal and Scipio*, published
in 1637 with a note on the title page that it had been acted in 1635, names
him as the actor who played Massinissa.

Act I

Enter PIERO *and* FUTELLI *at several doors.*

Piero. Accomplished man of fashion!
Futelli.   The times' wonder,
    Gallant of gallants, Genoa's Piero!
Piero. Italy's darling, Europe's joy, and so forth!
    The newest news, unvamped?
Futelli.   I am no foot-post,
    No pedlar of avisos, no monopolist   5
    Of forged corantos, monger of gazettes.
Piero. Monger of courtesans, fine Futelli;
    In certain kind a merchant of the staple
    For wares of use and trade; a taker-up,
    Rather indeed a knocker-down – the word   10
    Will carry either sense – but in pure earnest,
    How trolls the common noise?

ACT I [SCENE I].] *This ed.; ACTUS PRIMUS. Q. Q gives act divisions in Latin, but not scene divisions.*   7. fine Futelli] *Q*; my fine Futelli *Gifford.*

0.1. SD *at several doors*] The *Phoenix* appears to have had two doors leading out from the tiring-house and a discovery space in between them. Futelli and Piero each enter from a different door and presumably meet downstage.

4. *unvamped*] not patched or adapted. Piero's request is for unadorned gossip ('news'), in itself a paradox, since the point about gossip is that it tends to gather details as it spreads. A request for, or promise of, news often inauguarated a nonsense song or satire (Baskervill 59–68).

foot-post] messenger who carries news or letters on foot.

5. *avisos*] official dispatches or notifications.

6. *forged corantos*] newsletters full of inaccurate or invented information; forged in the sense of being of dubious credibility.

monger of gazettes] seller of news-sheets.

7. *courtesans*] prostitutes.

9. *taker-up*] Presumably in the sense of *OED* 4, 'a member of a gang of swindlers', but with a play on the sense of taking up the courtesans' skirts.

12. *trolls*] moves or circulates. Since 'to troll' is also to move the tongue (*OED* 4b), Piero's question might be translated as something like 'How wags the common tongue?'

46

Futelli.   Auria, who lately
    Wedded and bedded to the fair Spinella,
    Tired with the enjoyments of delights, is hasting
    To cuff the Turkish pirates in the service   15
    Of the great duke of Florence.
Piero.   Does not carry
    His pretty thing along?
Futelli.   Leaves her to buffet
    Land pirates here at home.
Piero.   That's thou and I,
    Futelli, sirrah, and Piero. Blockhead,
    To run from such an armful of pleasures   20
    For gaining what? A bloody nose of honour.
    Most sottish and abominable.
Futelli.   Wicked,
    Shameful, and cowardly, I will maintain.
Piero. Is all my signor's hospitality –
    Huge banquetings, deep revels, costly trappings –   25
    Shrunk to a cabin, and a single welcome
    To beverage and biscuit?
Futelli.   Hold thy peace, man.
    It makes for us – he comes; let's part demurely.
                                        [*They move aside.*]

14–16.] *Mislineated as prose in Q.*

17. *pretty thing*] Piero speaks of Spinella here as if she were a toy, with a clear play on her 'thing', that is, her sexual organ. He and Futelli both assume that Spinella will either fall prey to another man or men in Auria's absence or is at the least fair game.

27. *biscuit*] i.e. ship's biscuit, what Auria will have to eat in the 'cabin' to which he has now confined himself for his sea-journey.

28. *It makes for us –*] Futelli presumably means that Auria's absence will give him and Piero a chance to court Spinella, exactly as Camillo and Vespucci in *The Fancies, Chaste and Noble* take advantage of the temporary absence of Julio to harass his wife Flavia. He breaks off his remark at sight of Auria.

demurely] gravely, modestly. Since they have just been gossiping about his wife, they put on a serious look as Auria enters.

Enter ADURNI *and* AURIA.

Adurni. We wish thee, honoured Auria, life and safety.
    Return crowned with a victory whose wreath   30
    Of triumph may advance thy country's glory,
    Worthy your name and ancestors.
Auria.   My lord,
    I shall not live to thrive in any action
    Deserving memory when I forget
    Adurni's love and favour.
                    [*Piero and Futelli come forward.*]
Piero.   I present ye   35
    My service for a farewell; let few words
    Excuse all arts of compliment.
Futelli.   For my own part,
    Kill or be killed, for there's the short and long on't,
    Call me your shadow's hench-boy.
Auria.   Gentlemen,
    My business, urging on a present haste,   40
    Enforceth short reply.
Adurni.   We dare not hinder
    Your resolution, winged with thoughts so constant.
    All happiness!
Piero, Futelli.   Contents!
                [*Exeunt* ADURNI, PIERO, *and* FUTELLI.]

36.] *Gifford; Q has the speech prefix* FVL. *before* For my owne
part. 37–9.] *Gifford; Weber, following Q, gives from* For my own *to* hench-boy
to Fulgoso; Nogami gives it to Piero. 43.1.] *Weber. No exit is supplied in Q.*

36–7.] I follow Gifford's speech allocations here. Q has speech prefixes
for Futelli before 'Let few' and for Fulgoso before 'For my own part', which
Weber follows, adding an entrance for Fulgoso to allow him to be present
in the scene. It seems more likely, however, that Q's 'FVL.' is an error for
'FVT.', since Futelli's description of Fulgoso at 1.2.117–19 seems designed
to introduce him to the audience for the first time, and that something is
consequently amiss with the speech prefixes in this passage. It might be Auria
who says 'Let few words / Excuse all arts of compliment', but that can only
be conjecture.
    39. *hench-boy*] page of honour, often distinguished by a pleasing appear-
ance and manners.
    43.] a half-line.
    Contents] joys, satisfactions. Similarly at 2.2.77 and 2.2.103.

Auria. So leave the wintered people of the north
　　The minutes of their summer, when the sun　　　　45
　　Departing leaves them in cold robes of ice,
　　As I leave Genoa –

　　　　Enter TRELCATIO, SPINELLA, [*and*] CASTANNA.

　　　　　　now appears the object
　　Of my apprenticed heart. Thou bringst, Spinella,
　　A welcome in a farewell. Souls and bodies
　　Are severed for a time, a span of time,　　　　　50
　　To join again without all separation,
　　In a confirmèd unity for ever.
　　Such will our next embraces be for life;
　　And then to take the reck of our divisions
　　Will sweeten the remembrance of past dangers,　　55
　　Will fasten love in perpetuity,
　　Will force our sleeps to steal upon our stories.
　　These days must come, and shall, without a cloud
　　Or night of fear or envy. [*To Trelcatio*] To your charge,

47.1. and] *Gifford; & Q, where the SD appears in a marginal note besides ll.* 46,
47 *and* 48.　54. reck] *This ed.*; wrack *Q, Weber, Nogami*; wreck *Gifford, Keltie.*

---

44. *the . . . north*] People who live in the cold northern climes. Ford is most
likely to have been thinking of Muscovites, Icelanders or Sami, all of whom
had been encountered by English traders, sailors or explorers, particularly
Henry Hudson who in 1608 touched on Spitzbergen, Nova Zemlya and
Greenland. Ford might also have read Olaus Magnus's popular *Description
of the Northern Peoples* (1555) or George North's *Description of Swedland,
Gotland, and Finland* (1561), or have known of the Devon-born sea captain
Stephen Borough, who according to his 1584 tombstone in Chatham 'discovered Muscovia by the northerne sea passage to St. Nicholas in the yere
1553'.

51. *without all separation*] beyond or in a realm outside of the concept of
dividing the immaterial or spiritual from the material flesh: at the Last
Judgement, souls and bodies will be reunited for ever.

54. *reck*] heed, consideration (*OED* n.1), with an implication of mathe-
matical accounting or reckoning in regard to 'divisions'. 'To take the reck
of' would thus have something of the force of 'to take stock of' or 'to weigh
the impact of'. Neither Q's 'wrack' nor Gifford's 'wreck' makes sense, since
they will precisely *not* have been wrecked or damaged.

57. *force . . . stories*] compel our sleeping to overcome us by stealth while
we listen to our absorbing narratives.

59. *charge*] care, responsibility.

Trelcatio our good uncle, and the comfort   60
Of my Spinella's sister, fair Castanna,
I do entrust this treasure.
Trelcatio.   I dare promise
My husbanding that trust with truth and care.
Castanna. My sister shall to me stand an example
Of pouring free devotions for your safety.   65
Auria. Gentle Castanna, thou art a branch of goodness,
Grown on the self-same stock with my Spinella.
But why, my dear, hast thou locked up thy speech
In so much silent sadness? Oh, at parting
Belike one private whisper must be sighed!   70
Uncle, the best of peace enrich your family;
I take my leave.
Trelcatio.   Blessings and health preserve ye.   *Exit.*
Auria. Nay, nay, Castanna, you may hear our counsels;
A while you are designed your sister's husband.
Give me thy hand, Spinella; you did promise   75
To send me from you with more cheerful looks,
Without a grudge or tear; 'deed, love, you did.
Spinella. What friend have I left in your absence?
Auria.   Many.
Thy virtues are such friends, they cannot fail thee:
Faith, purity of thoughts, and such a meekness   80
As would force scandal to a blush.
Spinella.   Admit, sir,
The patent of your life should be called in,

---

62. *this treasure*] Spinella. The term is appropriate enough in terms of her being named after a jewel, but also suggesting the possibility that Auria, like Piero and Futelli, might perhaps regard her as a commodity.

65. *pouring*] Castanna derives her metaphor from the idea of pouring libations to the gods as a sign of piety and when offering a prayer.

free] generous, not stinted.

71–2.] Auria drops a hint to Trelcatio to leave so that he and Spinella may speak privately.

74.] *husband*] Companion, protector.

82.] your (God-given) entitlement to life should be revoked.

How am I left then to account with griefs,
More slaved to pity than a broken heart?
Auria, soul of my comforts! I let fall   85
No eye on breach of fortune; I contemn
No entertainment to divided hopes;
I urge no pressures by the scorn of change;
And yet, my Auria, when I but conceive
How easy 'tis, without impossibility,   90
Never to see thee more, forgive me then
If I conclude I may be miserable,
Most miserable.
Castanna.   And such conclusion, sister,
    Argues effects of a distrust more voluntary
    Than cause by likelihood.
Auria.   'Tis truth, Castanna.   95
Spinella. I grant it truth; yet, Auria, I'm a woman,
    And therefore apt to fear. To show my duty
    And not take heart from you, I'll walk from ye
    At your command, and not as much as trouble
    Your thought with one poor looking back.
Auria.   I thank thee,   100
    My worthy wife! Before we kiss, receive
    This caution from thine Auria; first – Castanna,
    Let us bid farewell.   [*Castanna walks aside.*]
Spinella.   Speak, good, speak.
Auria.   The steps
    Young ladies tread, left to their own discretion,

---

85. Auria, soul of my comforts!] *Gifford*; Auria! Soule of my comforts
Q.   96. I'm] *Weber*; I am *Q*.   98. not take heart] *Q*, *Nogami*; not to take
heart *Weber, Gifford*.   103.1.] *Gifford*.

---

83. *to account with griefs*] to come to terms with my woes. Given the
financial motive for Auria's departure and the fact that we will shortly hear
of Spinella losing a large sum of money, the financial metaphor is an appropriate one: she would be left in even greater poverty than they now find
themselves in, as well as being bereaved.
    84. *more . . . heart*] even more pitiable than if I had (merely) a broken
heart. The titles of two other Ford plays, *'Tis Pity She's a Whore* and *The
Broken Heart*, are suggestively evoked here.
    86. *breach*] assault, attack (*OED* n.4).
    contemn] despise.

However wisely printed, are observed   105
And construed as the lookers-on presume;
Point out thy ways then in such even paths
As thine own jealousies from others' tongues
May not intrude a guilt, though undeserved.
Admit of visits as of physic forced   110
Not to procure health, but for safe prevention
Against a growing sickness. In thy use
Of time and of discourse be found so thrifty
As no remembrance may impeach thy rest;
Appear not in a fashion that can prompt   115
The gazer's eye or holla to report
Some widowèd neglect of handsome value.
In recreations be both wise and free.
Live still at home, home to thyself; howe'er
Enriched with noble company, remember   120
A woman's virtue in her lifetime writes
The epitaph all covet on their tombs.
In short I know thou never wilt forget
Whose wife thou art, nor how upon thy lips
Thy husband at his parting sealed this kiss.   125

                                     [*He kisses her.*]

116. holla to report] *Nogami*; holla to report; *Q, Weber*; holla, to report *Gifford, Keltie*.   117. handsome] *Gifford*; hand, some *Q, Weber (missing line conj.)*.   125. sealed] *Weber (subst.)*; stald *Q*; stalled *Nogami*.

108. *As*] in such a way that.
108–9.] Spinella should behave so charily that she has no cause to imagine that people are talking about her.
110. *Admit of*] allow.
physic] medicine, cure.
114. *no ... rest*] no regret may stop you sleeping. Perhaps Auria is also thinking about Spinella's posthumous reputation.
116. *holla*] cry out.
117. *widowèd ... value*] failure to do what is proper because no longer under male supervision.
119. *to thyself*] alone.
119–22.] However good the company you might keep may be, it is virtue alone which leads to a good reputation after death. That keeping company is a danger to a woman's virtue, or at least to the general belief in it, is something of which Spinella will soon discover the truth.

　　　No more.

Spinella.   Dear heaven! – Go, sister, go.

　　　　　　　　　　Ex[eunt SPINELLA *and* CASTANNA].

Auria.   Done bravely,

And like the choice of glory. To know mine,

One of earth's best I have forgone.

　　　　　　　　　Enter AURELIO.

　　　　　　　　　　　　　　　See, see,

Yet in another I am rich; a friend,

A perfect one, Aurelio.

Aurelio.   Had I been   130

No stranger to your bosom, sir, ere now

You might have sorted me in your resolves

Companion of your fortunes.

Auria.   So the wrongs

I should have ventured on against thy fate

Must have denied all pardon. Not to hold   135

Dispute with reputations, why before

This present instant I concealed the stealth

Of my adventures from thy counsels, know

My wants do drive me hence.

Aurelio.   'Wants'? So you said,

And 'twas not friendly spoken.

Auria.   Hear me further.   140

---

126. SD] *Weber; Exit Q.*   127. glory. To] *This ed.; glory to Q.*   128.1.] *In Q*
the SD appears in a marginal note besides ll. 125–6.   138. thy] *Weber;* the *Q.*

126. *No more*] Either Auria is himself unable to say more or he wishes to
stop Spinella from prolonging the conversation.

Done bravely] Auria's approving comment on Spinella's behaviour fore-
shadows the way he puts her through her paces in the trial scene.

127–8.] Spinella has acted well and for the sake of glory. To secure his
own glory, Auria has deprived himself of one of the best people in the
world.

132. *sorted*] allotted, assigned.

resolves] resolutions.

133–5. *So . . . pardon*] Auria tells Aurelio that it would have been unpardonable to have involved his friend in his dangerous venture.

136. *reputations*] assessments, estimations (*OED* 1b). Auria does not want
a debate about his motive for concealment.

140. *friendly spoken*] said like a friend.

Aurelio. Auria, take heed the covert of a folly
  Willing to range: be not without excuse
  Discovered in the coinage of untruths.
  I use no harder language. Thou art near
  Already on a shipwreck in forsaking   145
  The holy land of friendship in forsaking
  To talk your wants. Fie!
Auria.   By that sacred thing
  Last issued from the temple where it dwelt,
  I mean our friendship, I am sunk so low
  In my estate that, bid me live in Genoa   150
  But six months longer, I survive the remnant
  Of all my store.
Aurelio.   Umph.
Auria.   In my country, friend –
  Where I have sided my superior, friend,
  Swayed opposition, friend – friend, here to fall
  Subject to scorn, or rarely found compassion,   155
  Were more than man that hath a soul could bear,
  A soul not stooped to servitude.

---

146. in forsaking] *Q*; and forbearing *conj. Gifford; missing line conj. Weber.*
Printer 'eyeskip' may have caused the repetition of the word from
145. 150. bid] *Weber*; bids *Q*.

141–2. *take . . . range*] Do not allow yourself to be carried away by your
foolish imagination. We see here the first indication that Aurelio is ready to
believe the worst of anybody; he thinks his friend may lie to him.
  141. *take heed*] beware of.
  covert] covering, something which offers concealment.
  143. *coinage*] counterfeiting.
  144. *harder*] more severe.
  145. *shipwreck*] destruction. Aurelio's metaphor uses Auria's desire for
travel against him.
  146. *holy land*] Judaea. Aurelio speaks of their friendship as if it were
sacramental, and Auria follows suit in his reply.
  153. *sided my superior*] walked or stood by the side of my betters. Auria
has held his own amongst his social superiors. The expression echoes
Huntly's words to Katherine in *Perkin Warbeck*, 'I am confident / Thou wilt
proportion all thy thoughts to side / Thy equals, if not equal thy superiors'
(1.2.112–14).
  153, 154. *friend*] Like the repetition of 'honest' Iago, Auria's insistence on
the term begins to sound ironic.
  154–6. *here . . . bear*] Even compassion would be difficult to bear, but it is
in any case unlikely to be found.

Aurelio.   You show
   Nor certainty, nor weak assurance yet
   Of reparation in this course, in case
   Command be proffered.
Auria.   He who cannot merit   160
   Preferment by employments, let him bare
   His throat unto the Turkish cruelty,
   Or die or live a slave without redemption.
Aurelio. For that, so; but you have a wife, a young,
   A fair wife; she, though she could never claim   165
   Right in prosperity, was never tempted
   By trial of extremes, to youth and beauty
   Baits for dishonour and a perished fame.
Auria. Show me the man that lives, and to my face
   Dares speak, scarce think, such tyranny against   170
   Spinella's constancy, except Aurelio –
   He is my friend.
Aurelio.   There lives not then a friend
   Dares love you like Aurelio, that Aurelio
   Who, late and early, often said and truly
   Your marriage with Spinella would entangle   175
   As much th'opinion due to your discretion
   As your estate; it hath done so to both.
Auria. I find it hath.
Aurelio.   He who prescribes no law,
   No limits of condition, to the objects
   Of his affection, but will merely wed   180

---

157. You] *Weber;* Your *Q.*

157–60. *You … proferred*] Aurelio objects that, even if Auria is given greater military responsibility ('command'), he has given no indication of how this will or might help his finances.

159. *reparation*] putting right, restoring.

161. *preferment*] advancement, promotion.

162.] The Turks were a byword for savagery in the period, and many Italian city-states were in semi-permanent conflict with Ottoman navies.

165. *A fair wife*] Aurelio's phrase recalls Michael Cassio in *Othello*, who according to Iago is 'A fellow almost damn'd in a fair wife' (1.1.21).

172.] With each repetition, 'friend' takes on a more hostile and aggressive edge.

175–7.] Marrying Spinella has compromised both Auria's finances and his reputation for wisdom.

A face because 'tis round, or limned by nature
In purest red and white, or, at the best,
For that his mistress owes an excellence
Of qualities, knows when and how to speak,
Where to keep silence, with fit reasons why,   185
Whose virtues are her only dower, else none
In either kind, ought of himself to master
Such fortunes as add fuel to their loves,
For otherwise – but herein I am idle,
Have fooled to little purpose.
Auria.   She's my wife.   190
Aurelio. And being so, it is not manly done
To leave her to the trial of her wits,
Her modesty, her innocence, her vows.
This is the way that points her out an art
Of wanton life.
Auria.   Sir, said ye?
Aurelio.   You form reasons,   195
Just ones, for your abandoning the storms
Which threaten your own ruin, but propose
No shelter for her honour. What my tongue
Hath uttered, Auria, is but honest doubt,
And you are wise enough in the construction.   200
Auria. Necessity must arm my confidence,
Which if I live to triumph over, friend,
And e'er come back in plenty, I pronounce
Aurelio heir of what I can bequeath;

---

186. else none] *Gifford*; else *Q, Nogami; missing line or lines conj. Weber, Keltie.*

181. *limned*] adorned, decorated (literally painted).
186. *dower*] Usually the portion of a deceased husband's estate reserved for his wife, but could also be the money the wife brought to the husband. Spinella's virtues are all she has.
187–8. *ought . . . loves*] should himself have enough money to provide the material support which will keep their love strong.
190. *fooled*] talked aimlessly.
203–4.] Such apparently excessive generosity on the part of the husband towards his friend is also found in *A Woman Killed with Kindness* and to a lesser extent in *Arden of Faversham*, and is also comparable to Othello's excessive trust in Iago. Collectively, these parallels work to mislead the audience by inviting them to read events in terms of the familiar genre of domestic tragedy, and expect a tragic outcome.

Some fit deduction for a worthy widow   205
Allowed, with caution she be like to prove so.
Aurelio. Who? I your heir? Your wife being yet so young,
In every probability so forward
To make you a father? Leave such thoughts.
Auria.   Believe it,
Without replies, Aurelio. Keep this note,   210
A warrant for receiving from Martino
Two hundred ducats; as you find occasion
Dispose them in my absence to Spinella.
I would not trust her uncle; he, good man,
Is at an ebb himself. Another hundred   215
I left with her, a fourth I carry with me.
Am I not poor, Aurelio, now? Exchange
Of more debates between us would undo
My resolution. Walk a little, prithee;
Friends we are, and will embrace; but let's not speak   220
Another word.
Aurelio.   I'll follow you to your horse.   *Ex[eunt].*

---

205. *fit deduction*] suitable sum set aside.

206. *with . . . so*] provided that she does appear likely to prove worthy. Auria here seems also to have some doubts about Spinella.

207-9.] We never hear anything more of the possibility that Spinella might be pregnant, though it might have a bearing on the question of her fainting (5.2.47, 142). The fact that it is not mentioned need not rule out the possibility: the audience never has any idea that Anne Frankford in *A Woman Killed with Kindness* has been pregnant until they hear of her having given birth to two children.

208. *forward*] likely.

212. *Two hundred ducats*] A substantial sum of money. Auria clearly places great reliance on Aurelio's judgement and trustworthiness.

215. *Is at an ebb himself*] Another example of the play's interest in seafaring imagery, and an indication that this is a generally cash-strapped society.

215-16. *Another hundred | I left with her*] This sum is presumably the money that we later discover Spinella to have been gambling with.

[ACT I SCENE 2]

Enter ADURNI *and* FUTELLI. [ADURNI *is holding*]
a letter.

Adurni. With her own hand?
Futelli.   She never used, my lord,
A second means, but kissed the letter first,
O'erlooked the superscription; then let fall
Some amorous drops, kissed it again, talked to it
Twenty times over, set it to her mouth,   5
Then gave it me, then snatched it back again,
Then cried 'Oh my poor heart!', and in an instant
'Commend my truth and secrecy'. Such medley
Of passion yet I never saw in woman.
Adurni. In woman? Th'art deceived; but that we both   10
Had mothers, I could say how women are,
In their own natures, models of mere change,
Of change of what is naught to what is worse.
She fee'd ye liberally?
Futelli.   Twenty ducats
She forced on me; vowed by the precious love   15
She bore the 'best of men' (I use, my lord,
Her very words), 'the miracle of men,
Malfato' (then she sighed), this 'mite of gold'
Was 'only entrance to a farther bounty'.
'Tis meant, my lord, belike press-money.

0.1. SD ADURNI *is holding*] *This ed.; Enter Adurni and Futelli. A letter Q.*
14. fee'd] *Gifford*; fed *Q.*

---

1. *With her own hand?*] Adurni may be surprised to learn that Levidolce is literate. This was not something that could be assumed of women from below the upper classes.
　2. *means*] agent or instrument.
　3. *O'erlooked*] looked over.
superscription] heading or address.
　4. *amorous drops*] tears of love.
　12. *models*] epitomes, exemplars. Women, like the moon by which they were thought to be governed, were thought to be fickle and changeable.
　14. *fee'd*] paid.
　18. *mite*] small coin of low value. The biblical story of the widow's mite – a small sum, but all she had, so she was rewarded – may be ironically glanced at: Levidolce has divorced her husband and is far from acting virtuously, but this action will in fact set in train reformation and reconciliation for her.
　20. *belike*] probably.
　20. *press-money*] money paid to a soldier or sailor when forced to enlist. Futelli supposes that Levidolce plans to enlist him in her service.

Adurni.   Devil!   20
    How durst she tempt thee, Futelli, knowing
    Thy love to me?
Futelli.   There lies, my lord, her cunning,
    Rather her craft. First she began what pity
    It was that men should differ in estates
    Without proportion – some so strangely rich,   25
    Others so miserable poor. 'And yet',
    Quoth she, 'since 'tis very deed unfit
    All should be equals, so I must confess
    It were good justice that the properest men
    Should be preferred to fortune, such as nature   30
    Had marked with fair abilities; of which
    Genoa, for aught I know, hath wondrous few,
    Not two to boast of'.
Adurni.   Here began her itch.
Futelli. I answered, she was happy then, whose choice
    In you, my lord, was singular.
Adurni.   Well urged.   35
Futelli. She smiled, and said, it might be so, and yet –
    There stopped. Then I closed with her, and concluded
    The title of a lord was not enough
    For absolute perfection: I had seen
    Persons of meaner quality much more   40
    Exact in fair endowments – but your lordship
    Will pardon me, I hope.
Adurni.   And love thee for it.
Futelli. 'Phew! Let that pass,' quoth she, 'and now we prattle
    Of handsome gentlemen, in my opinion
    Malfato is a very pretty fellow,   45
    Is he not, pray, sir?' I had then the truth

20–2.] *Weber; mislineated as prose in* Q.   21. thee] *Q*; thee [thus] *Gifford.*
27. 'tis very deed] *Q*; 'tis [in] very deed *Weber, Gifford, Nogami (subst.).*

---

27. *very deed*] truly; a shortened form of 'in very deed'.
29. *properest*] most handsome and well-made.
33. *itch*] lustful desire.
43. *Phew*] huh. 'Phew' is identified by Dugdale Sykes as 'a common interjection in Ford' and possible marker of his hand (Sargeaunt 47); cf. *Love's Sacrifice* 5.1.136, *The Lover's Melancholy* 1.2.105, and *Perkin Warbeck* 1.1.132.

Of what I roved at, and with more than praise
Approved her judgement in so high a strain,
Without comparison, my honoured lord,
That soon we both concluded of the man,   50
The match, and business.
Adurni.   For delivering
A letter to Malfato?
Futelli.   Whereto I
No sooner had consented, with protests –
I did protest, my lord – of secrecy
And service, but she kissed me, as I live,   55
Of her own free accord – I trust your lordship
Conceives not me amiss. Pray rip the seal,
My lord; you'll find sweet stuff, I dare believe.
                                    Adurni reads.
Adurni. 'Present to the most accomplished of men, Malfato,
    with this love a service'.
Kind superscription! Prithee find him out;   60
Deliver it with compliment. Observe
How ceremoniously he does receive it.
Futelli. Will not your lordship peruse the contents?
Adurni. Enough! I know too much. Be just and cunning.
A wanton mistress is a common sewer;   65
Much newer project labours in my brain –

59.] *This ed.; three lines in* Q.   66. Much newer] *Gifford*; Much never *Q*;
Must never *Weber*.

47. *roved at*] was getting at.
48. *strain*] vein, style of expression.
49. *Without*] beyond.
50. *concluded on*] reached a decision about.
57. *Conceives me not amiss*] does not think ill of me.
58. *sweet stuff*] fine old nonsense.
62. *How ceremoniously*] with what degree of respect.
64. *cunning*] This word had an apparently pejorative sense when used of
Levidolce at l. 22, but it is a quality that Adurni wants to see in Futelli.
65.] An unfaithful lover is like a public sewer (that is, anyone can deposit
bodily fluids in her).

Enter PIERO.

Your friend! Here's now the Gemini of wit;
What odd conceit is next on foot, some cast
Of neat invention, ha, sirs?
Piero.   Very fine,
I do protest, my lord.
Futelli.   Your lordship's ear   70
Shall share i'th' plot.
Adurni.   As how?
Piero.   You know, my lord,
Young Amoretta, old Trelcatio's daughter –
An honest man, but poor.
Futelli.   And, my good lord,
He that is honest must be poor, my lord,
It is a common rule.
Adurni.   Well, Amoretta.   75
Pray one at once: my knowledge is not much;
Of her instruct me.
Piero.   Speak, Futelli.
Futelli.   Spare me.
Piero has the tongue more pregnant.
Piero.   Fie,
Play on your creature.
Futelli.   Shall be yours.
Piero.   Nay, good.
Adurni. Well, keep your mirth, my dainty honeys; agree   80
Some two days hence, till when –
Piero.   By any means
Partake the sport, my lord: this thing of youth –

66.1.] *Weber; this is placed after line 68 in Q.*   70–1. ear / Shall] *Gifford*; ear
shall *Q*; care / Shall *Weber.*   78–9. Fie, / Play] *Weber (subst.)*; Fie play *Q.*

67. *Gemini*] twin, other half.
68. *on foot*] under way, in process.
cast] device, trick (*OED* n.24).
76. *Pray one at once*] one at a time, please.
78. *pregnant*] resourceful, full of ideas.
79. *creature*] servant, dependant.
Shall be yours] you're the one to say it.
Nay, good] No, sir.
82. *partake*] share.

Futelli. Handsome enough, good face, quick eye, well bred –
Piero. Is yet possessed so strangely –
Futelli.   With an humour
    Of thinking, she deserves –
Piero.   A duke, a count,   85
    At least a viscount, for her husband that –
Futelli. She scorns all mention of a match beneath
    One of the foresaid nobles; will not ride
    In a caroche without eight horses.
Piero.   Six,
    She may be drawn to; four –
Futelli.   Are for the poor;   90
    But for two horses in a coach –
Piero.   She says,
    Th'are not for creatures of heaven's making; fitter –
Futelli. Fitter for litters to convey hounds in
    Than people Christian; yet herself –
Piero.   Herself
    Walks evermore afoot, and knows not whether   95
    A coach doth trot or amble –
Futelli.   But by hearsay.
Adurni. Stop, gentlemen, you run a-gallop both;
    Are out of breath sure. 'Tis a kind of compliment
    Scarce entered to the times, but certainly
    You coin a humour. Let me understand   100
    Deliberately your fancy.

84–5. humour/ Of] *Weber*; humour of *Q*. 89–90. Six / She] *Weber*; six she
Q. 90. poor] *Weber*; power *Q*. 94–5. Herself / Walks] *Weber*; Herselfe
walkes *Q*.

---

89. *caroche*] coach or chariot of a luxurious kind.

93. *litters to convey hounds in*] small platform-like carriages, usually sup-
ported on poles resting on men's shoulders, in which a person or animal
could lie.

95–6. *whether ... amble*] whether a coach is moving quickly or slowly. The
coach itself cannot in fact do either of these things; the horses pulling it have
to. Piero seems to imply that Amoretta's inexperience of coaches is so total
that she could not even describe the movement of one accurately.

99. *Scarce entered to*] hardly creditable to.

100. *coin a humour*] invent a new sort of wit, perhaps with a suggestion
of doing so illegitimately, since to coin can be to counterfeit.

101. *Deliberately*] systematically.

fancy] conceit (in the sense of odd-seeming metaphor used by the metaphysical poets), whimsical plan.

Piero.   In plain troth,
    My lord, the she whom we describe is such,
    And lives here, here in Genoa, this city,
    This very city, now, the very now.
Adurni. Trelcatio's daughter?
Futelli.   Has refusèd suitors   105
    Of worthy rank, substantial and free parts,
    Only for that they are not dukes, or counts;
    Yet she herself, with all her father's store,
    Can hardly weigh above four hundred ducats.
Adurni. Now your design for sport?
Piero.   Without prevention: 110
    Guzman, the Spaniard late cashiered, most gravely
    Observes the full punctilios of his nation,
    And him have we beleaguered to accost
    This she-piece under a pretence of being
    Grandee of Spain and cousin to twelve princes.   115
Futelli. For rival unto whom we have enraged
    Fulgoso, the rich coxcomb lately started
    A gentleman out of a sutler's hut
    In the late Flemish wars. We have resolved him
    He is descended from Pantagruel   120
    Of famous memory by the father's side,
    And by the mother from Dame Fusti-Bunga,

---

106. *substantial*] of substance, wealthy.
free parts] generous qualities.
110. *prevention*] delay, impediment.
111. *cashiered*] dismissed from service.
112. *punctilios*] formalities, niceties.
113. *beleaguered*] laid siege to.
accost] court, pay addresses to.
114. *she-piece*] female fortress (*OED* 11b).
117–18. *lately . . . gentleman*] recently catapulted to gentlemanly status.
117. *coxcomb*] fool.
118. *sutler's hut*] hut of one who sells provisions to soldiers.
119. *late Flemish wars*] The Thirty Years War, which had broken out in 1618 and was not to finish until 1648, allowed the Dutch to throw off the hated rule of the Spanish. Ford had dedicated *The Broken Heart* to William, Lord Craven, a prominent figure in it.
120. *Pantagruel*] One of the giants in Rabelais' *La Vie de Gargantua et de Pantagruel* first published in England in 1567.
122. *Fusti-Bunga*] Nogami suggests 'possibly Ford's coinage out of "fusty" and "bungy"' and glosses it as 'a female personification of a hugely swollen, smelly cask' (270).

Who, troubled long time with a strangury,
Vented at last salt-water so abundantly
As drowned the land 'twixt Zieriksee and Veere,   125
Where steeples' tops are only seen. He casts
Beyond the moon, and will be greater yet
In spite of don.
Adurni.   You must abuse the maid
Beyond amends.
Futelli.   But countenance the course,
My lord, and it may chance, beside the mirth,   130
To work a reformation on the maiden.
Her father's leave is granted, and thanks promised.
Our ends are harmless trials.
Adurni.   I betray no
Secrets of such use.
Both.   Your lordship's humblest.
                                        Exeunt.

[ACT I SCENE 3]

Enter AURELIO *and* MALFATO.

Aurelio. A melancholy grounded and resolved,
Received into a habit, argues love,
Or deep impression of strong discontents.
In cases of these rarities a friend
Upon whose faith and confidence we may   5
Vent with security our grief becomes
Ofttimes the best physician; for, admit

---

128. must] *Q*; much *conj. Gifford.*   133. betray no] *Gifford*; betray me *Q*;
betray / No *Weber*; betray not *Nogami.*   134. Exeunt] *Gifford*; Exit *Q.*

123. *strangury*] a disease of the urinary organs.
124. *Vented*] emitted.
125. *Zieriksee*] town in Zeeland province in the Netherlands.
Veere] port town, also in Zeeland.
126. *He...moon*] he aspires higher than the moon.
128. *In spite of don*] To annoy the supposed Spanish grandee.
129. *countenance*] give your blessing to.
131. *reformation*] cure, improvement.
133. *harmless trials*] apparent ordeals which are merely playful; cf the main
plot, in which Spinella is 'tried'.
Secrets of such use] secrets so trivial.

We find no remedy, we cannot miss
Advice instead of comfort, and believe
It is an ease, Malfato, to disburden   10
Our souls of secret clogs, where they may find
A rest in pity, though not in redress.
Malfato. Let all this sense be yielded to.
Aurelio.   Perhaps
You measure what I say the common nature
Of an officious curiosity.   15
Malfato. Not I, sir.
Aurelio.   Or that other private ends
Sift your retirements –
Malfato.   Neither.

                         Enter FUTELLI.

Futelli.   Under favour,
Signor Malfato, I am sent to crave
Your leisure for a word or two in private.
Malfato. To me! Your mind?
Futelli.   This letter will inform ye.   20
Malfato. Letter? How's this? What's here?
Futelli.   Speak ye to me, sir?
Malfato. Brave riddle! I'll endeavour to unfold it.
Aurelio. [*To Futelli*] How fares the Lord Adurni?
Futelli.   Sure, in health, sir.
Aurelio. He is a noble gentleman, withal
Happy in his endeavours. The general voice   25
Sounds him for courtesy, behaviour, language,
And every fair demeanour, an example.

13–14.] *Weber; prose in Q.*

11. *clogs*] loads.
21.] Malfato (who is later seen not to be quick-witted) either fails to grasp what Futelli is offering him and promps a sarcastic response from him, or is possibly not speaking clearly because he is distracted by reading the letter, so that Futelli is therefore genuinely unsure if he is being addressed or not.
24. *withal*] in addition.
25–6. *general . . . him*] public opinion speaks of him as.

Titles of honour add not to his worth,
Who is himself an honour to his titles.
Malfato. You know from whence this comes?
Futelli. [*Laughs.*]   I do.
Malfato.   D'ee laugh!   30
But that I must consider such as spaniels
To those who feed and clothe them, I would print
Thy panderism upon thy forehead. There,
Bear back that paper to the hell from whence
It gave thee thy directions. Tell this lord   35
He ventured on a foolish policy
In aiming at the scandal of my blood.
The trick is childish, base, say base!
Futelli.   You wrong him.
Aurelio. Be wise, Malfato.
Malfato.   Say, I know this whore.
She who sent this temptation was wife   40
To his abusèd servant, and divorced
From poor Benazzi, senseless of the wrongs,
That Madam Levidolce and Adurni
Might revel in their sports without control,
Secure, unchecked.
Aurelio.   You range too wildly now,   45
Are too much inconsiderate.

28–9.] Ford often expresses scepticism about the value of titles *per se*, as in the Dedicatory Epistle to *Perkin Warbeck*: 'Eminent titles may indeed inform who their owners are, not often what'.

30.] 'D'ee' (for 'do thee' or 'do ye') is a distinctive form in Ford, perhaps originating in his Devonshire background.

31. *But that I must*] if I didn't have to.

32–3. *print . . . forehead*] slash your forehead to brand you a pimp. Though not a standard punishment for pimps, marking of the face is sometimes associated with sexual misdemeanours, as when the adulterious Anne Frankford in Heywood's *A Woman Killed with Kindness* begs her husband not to mark her face.

37. *the scandal of my blood*] the bringing of scandal on my blood. Blood, a recurrent word in Ford, suggests both Malfato's house and kinship group, which would suffer by association from any disgrace which fell upon him, and also his own blood, which in Renaissance thought would be seen as the source of the lust which had supposedly motivated him, as when Richardetto in *'Tis Pity She's a Whore* says that Annabella's sickness is caused by 'a fullness of her blood' (3.4.8), meaning that she has an unsatisfied readiness for sex.

Malfato.   I am
      A gentleman free-born. I never wore
      The rags of any great man's looks, nor fed
      Upon their after-meals. I never crouched
      Unto the offal of an office promised   50
      Reward for long attendance, and then missed.
      I read no difference between this huge,
      This monstrous big word lord, and gentleman,
      More than the title sounds; for aught I learn,
      The latter is as noble as the first;   55
      I'm sure more ancient.
Aurelio.   Let me tell you then,
      You are too bitter, talk you know not what:
      Make all men equals, and confound all course
      Of order, and of nature? This is madness.
Malfato. 'Tis so; and I have reason to be mad;   60
      Reason, Aurelio, by my truth and hopes.
      This wit Futelli brings a suit of love
      From Levidolce, one, however masked
      In colourable privacy, is famed
      The Lord Adurni's pensioner, at least.   65
      Am I a husband picked out for a strumpet,
      For a cast-suit of bawdry? Aurelio,
      You are as I am; you could ill digest
      The trial of a patience so unfit.
      Begone, Futelli! Do not mince one syllable   70
      Of what you hear. Another fetch like this
      May tempt a peace to rage; so say, begone.
Futelli. I shall report your answer.   *Exit.*

---

47. *free-born*] not born into slavery and hence entitled by birth to all the
rights of a citizen.

56. *more ancient*] of longer standing, and hence worthier of respect.
Malfato is no parvenu, or in Renaissance terms no 'mushroom', sprung up
overnight. Anyone with money could buy a baronetcy or a peerage (as in
The Alchemist where Face promises Kastri! that one of Subtle's familiars
can earn him 'Enough to buy a barony' (3.4.60) within a fortnight), but a
gentleman had to come of a gentle family.

64. *colourable*] able to provide camouflage.

67. *cast-suit*] discarded clothing; metaphorically, unwanted mistress.

70. *mince*] make light of, minimise.

71. *fetch*] dodge, trick.

Malfato.   What have I
    Deserved to be so used? In colder blood
    I do confess nobility requires   75
    Duty and love; it is a badge of virtue,
    By action first acquired, and next in rank
    Unto anointed royalty. Wherein
    Have I neglected distance, or forgot
    Observance to superiors? Sure, my name   80
    Was in the note mistook.
Aurelio.   We will consider
    The meaning of this mystery.
Malfato.   Not so.
    Let them fear bondage who are slaves to fear;
    The sweetest freedom is an honest heart.

                                                          Exeunt.

81–2.] *Weber; Aurelio's speech is all on one line in Q.*

Act 2

ACT 2 [SCENE I]

Enter FUTELLI *and* GUZMAN.

Futelli. Dexterity and sufferance, brave don,
    Are engines the pure politic must work with.
Guzman. We understand.
Futelli.   In subtleties of war –
    I talk t'ee now in your own occupation,
    Your trade, or what you please: unto a soldier –   5
    Surprisal of an enemy by stratagem
    Or downright cutting throats is all one thing.
Guzman. Most certain. On, proceed.
Futelli.   By way of parallel,
    You drill or exercise your company,
    No matter which for terms, before you draw   10
    Into the field; so in the feats of courtship,
    First choice is made of thoughts, behaviour, words,
    The set of looks, the posture of the beard,
    Beso las manos, cringes of the knee,
    The very hums and hahs, thumps, and ay mes.   15
Guzman. We understand all these; advance.
Futelli.   Then next,
    Your enemy in face – your mistress, mark it –
    Now you consult either to skirmish slightly,

ACT 2 [SCENE I].] *This ed.; Actus Secundus. Q.*

---

2. *politic*] politician.

10. *No . . . terms*] whichever of those terms you prefer to use.

14. *Beso las manos*] Spanish for hand-kissing. The phrase '*bezolus manus*' is found in Jonson's *The Alchemist* (4.3.21) and in Massinger's *The Great Duke of Florence*, which was also acted at the Phoenix and printed in 1636 with a commendatory poem by Ford (4.1, sig. Gv).

cringes of the knee] bending one's knee as when curtsying.

15.] Futelli lists a variety of sighing noises and gestures which would be an expected part of the lover's repertoire. 'Hums and hahs' are sighs and groans; 'thumps' are presumably blows which he gives himself in the region of the heart; 'ay mes' are lamentations.

That's careless amours, or to enter battle,
Then fall to open treaty, or to work   20
By secret spies or gold. Here you corrupt
The chambermaid, a fatal engine, or
Place there an ambuscado – that's contract
With some of her near friends for half her portion –
Or offer truce, and in the interim,   25
Run upon slaughter – 'tis a noble treachery –
That's swear and lie, steal her away; and to her
Cast caps, and cry '*Victoria!*' The field's
Thine own, my don, she's thine.
Guzman.   We do vouchsafe her.
Futelli. Hold her then fast.
Guzman.   As fast as can the arms   30
Of strong imagination hold her.
Futelli.   No,
She's skipped your hold; my imagination's eyes
Perceives she not endures the touch or scent
Of your war-overworn habiliments,
Which I forgot in my instructions   35
To warn you of. Therefore, my warlike don,
Apparel speedily your imagination
With a more courtly outside.
Guzman.   'Tis soon done.

31–2. No, / She's] *Weber (subst.)*; No, sh'as *Q*.   32. skipped] *Q (skipt)*; scap'd *conj. Dyce*.

---

22. *engine*] tool. To bribe Amoretta's chambermaid might make her endorse the cause of a particular lover or reveal her mistress's tastes and preferences.
23. *ambuscado*] ambush.
23–4. *contract...portion*] do a deal with some of her (Amoretta's) close relatives for half of her dowry.
27. *steal her away*] abduct her. This could be a prelude to a forced marriage, as when the Earl of Bothwell abducted Mary, Queen of Scots and she subsequently felt compelled to marry him.
28. *Cast caps*] toss hats in the air.
30. *arms*] Guzman puns on his own arms and on the weapons which he has imagined himself using in his military-style campaign against Amoretta.
34. *war-overworn*] made shabby by war. This is the first of a number of references to the poor state of Guzman's garments. In *The Rogue*, Guzman de Alfarache is always careful to describe his wardrobe in great detail.
habiliments] clothes.

Futelli. As soon as said; in all the clothes thou hast,
    More than that walking wardrobe on thy back.   40
Guzman. Imagine first our rich mockado doublet,
    With our cut cloth-of-gold sleeves, and our quellio,
    Our diamond-buttoned calamanco hose,
    Our plume of ostrich, with the embroidered scarf
    The Duchess Infantasgo rolled our arm in.   45
Futelli. Ay, this is brave indeed.
Guzman.   Our cloak whose cape is
    Larded with pearls, which the Indian caciques
    Presented to our countryman De Cortés
    For ransom of his life, rated in value
    At thirteen thousand pistolets – the guerdon   50

---

47. caciques] *This ed.*; Iacquies *Q*; cacique *Gifford*; lackies *Weber*.

39–40.] Futelli implies that it doesn't take Guzman long to imagine himself dressed in every garment he owns because he has very little more than he is already wearing.

41. *mockado*] inferior version of velvet.

42. *quellio*] Spanish ruff.

43. *calamanco*] woollen material from Flanders, glossy on one side and chequered on the other.

hose] clothing worn on the leg, sometimes also covering the foot, like stockings, and sometimes not, like gaiters.

45. *The Duchess Infantasgo*] The Duke of Infantasgo is named in Anthony Copley's *Wits, fittes and fancies*, a possible source for the play (**see pp. 9–11**) and also in *Sir Walter Raleigh's Ghost; or England's Forewarner* (Utrecht: printed by John Schellem, 1626). Despite being published in Utrecht, the book is in English, and Ford's interest in Ralegh, whose trial had been presided over by his great-uncle Sir John Popham, might well have drawn it to his attention. The duke of Infantasgo is there mentioned in the same breath as the duke of Lerma, hero of *The Great Favourite, or the Duke of Lerma*, a post-Restoration play ostensibly by Sir Robert Howard which appears to be a palimpsest incorporating an earlier core which may well have been by Ford.

rolled our arm in] wrapped round our arm. (Guzman is using the royal we.)

47. *Larded with*] thickly smeared with. Lard is pork fat, so again there is a suggestion of the unsavoury and the smelly about Guzman's clothes.

caciques] Native American leaders. Ford may be thinking of the conquistador Nuño Beltrán de Guzmán (see Introduction, **p. 8**) when he makes his Guzman an associate of De Cortés.

48. *De Cortés*] Hernán Cortés or Cortez (1485–1547), the famous conquistador.

50. *pistolets*] Spanish gold coins.

guerdon] reward.

Of our achievement when we rescued
The Infanta from the boar in single duel,
Near to the Austrian forest, with this rapier,
This only, very, naked, single rapier.
Futelli. Top and topgallant brave!
Guzman.   We will appear   55
Before our Amoretta like the issue
Of our progenitors.
Futelli.   Imagine so,
And that this rich suit of imagination
Is on already now (which is most probable)
As that apparel. Here stands your Amoretta;   60
Make your approach and court her.
Guzman.   Lustre of beauty,
Not to affright your tender soul with horror,
We may descend to tales of peace and love,
Soft whispers fitting ladies' closets; for
Thunder of cannon, roaring smoke and fire,   65
As if hell's maw had vomited confusion,
The clash of steel, the neighs of barbèd steeds,
Wounds spouting blood, towns capering in the air,
Castles pushed down, and cities ploughed with swords
Become great Guzman's oratory best,   70
Who, though victorious – and during life
Must be – yet now grants parley to thy smiles.

55. brave!] *Weber*; brave, *Q.*   59–60. probable) / As that apparel] *This ed.*;
probable / As that apparel) *Q.*

55. *Top and topgallant brave*] in the height of fashion. The topsail and
topgallant sail were used to give extra speed, so the expression 'top and
topgallant' comes to mean in full career (*OED* top n.1, 9c).
56. *issue*] offspring.
56–7. *like ... progenitors*] as befits one descended from my ancestors.
60. *Here ... Amoretta*] Futelli impersonates Amoretta so that Guzman can
practise courting as 'Ganymede' in *As You Like It* pretends to impersonate
Rosalind.
64. *Soft ... closets*] Gentle whispering of the sort that is suitable for ladies'
most intimate rooms.
68. *towns capering in the air*] Cf. Marlowe, *Tamburlaine the Great*, Part 2,
3.2.61, 'and make whole cities caper in the air'. Like Ancient Pistol, Guzman
presumably thinks that aping Tamburlaine's rhetoric will make him sound
valiant.

Futelli. 'Sfoot, don, you talk too big! You make her tremble.
    Do you not see't imaginarily?
    I do, as plainly as you saw the death   75
    Of the Austrian boar. She rather hears
    Of feasting than of fighting; take her that way.
Guzman. Yes, we will feast, my queen, my empress, saint;
    Shalt taste no delicates but what are dressed
    With costlier spices than the Arabian bird   80
    Sweetens her funeral bed with. We will riot
    With every change of meats, which may renew
    Our blood unto a spring so pure, so high,
    That from our pleasures shall proceed a race
    Of sceptre-bearing princes, who at once   85
    Must reign in every quarter of the globe.
Futelli. [*Aside*] Can more be said by one that feeds on herring
    And garlic constantly?
Guzman.   Yes, we will feast –
Futelli. Enough, she's taken, and will love you now,
    As well in buff as your imagined bravery.   90
    Your dainty ten-times-dressed buff, with this language,
    Bold man of arms, shall win upon her, doubt not,
    Beyond all silken puppetry. Think no more
    Of your mockados, calamancoes, quellios,
    Pearl-larded capes and diamond-buttoned breeches.   95
    Leave such poor outside helps to puling lovers,
    Such as Fulgoso, your weak rival, is,
    That starveling-brained companion. Appear you

---

73. *'Sfoot*] By God's foot, a mild oath.

79. *delicates*] delicacies, items of food that are particularly fine. Guzman's extravagant promises in this speech echo those of Sir Epicure Mammon in *The Alchemist* when he is wooing Dol.

80. *the Arabian bird*] the mythical phoenix, famous for being unique. At the end of its life, it supposedly made itself a funeral pyre enriched with the spices for which Arabia was celebrated, such as saffron, cinnamon, cardamom and cloves. The sun would set light to this and the phoenix would fan it with its wings. Finally the bird itself would go up in flames, only to be reborn from the ashes.

90. *buff*] leather of which military jerkins were made, which forms a sad contrast to the much richer garments of Guzman's imagination. Futelli suggests that Guzman's rhetoric is so powerful that his clothes will not matter.

96. *puling*] whining.

98. *starveling*] ill-nourished, emaciated.

At first (at least) in your own warlike fashion.
I pray be ruled, and change not a thread about you.   100
Guzman. The humour takes, for I, sir, am a man
Affects not shifts; I will adventure thus.
Futelli. Why, so you carry her from all the world.
I'm proud my stars designed me out an instrument
In such an high employment.
Guzman.   Gravely spoken;   105
You may be proud on't –

Enter FULGOSO *and* PIERO.

Fulgoso.   What is lost is lost,
Money is trash, and ladies are et ceteras,
Play's play, luck's luck, fortune's an I-know-what.
You see the worst of me, and – what's all this now?
Piero. A very spark, I vow; you will be styled   110
Fulgoso the invincible! But did
The fair Spinella lose an equal part?
How much in all, d'ee say?
Fulgoso.   Bare threescore ducats,
Thirty a piece; we need not care who know it.
She played, I went her half, walked by, and whistled   115
After my usual manner thus –   *Whistles*
               unmoved,
As no such thing had ever been, as it were,

---

116. *Whistles*] *Weber; marginal in* Q.

101–2. *a man / Affects not shifts*] a man [who] is not fond of changing his clothing.
106. *What...lost*] Fulgoso has been gaming, which is the first thing Guzman de Alfarache, the eponymous hero of *The Rogue*, does when he pays his second visit to Genoa to be avenged on his uncle and kinsmen for his treatment during his first visit (Alemán 3, pp. 346–7).
107. *et ceteras*] so forths. Fulgoso perhaps fails to finish the sentence because he notices he has company, but, like 'I-know-what' in the next line, '*et ceteras*' is clearly a euphemism for whore(s).
110. *spark*] witty young man.
115. *whistled*] As a sign of indifference to his loss. Fulgoso might also indicate by look or gesture his feelings about the men who have taken his money and the woman who has helped him lose it; certainly the whole scene has a sleazy atmosphere which encourages us to think ill of Spinella (cf. *The Fancies Chaste and Noble*, where all the women are subtly incriminated before being finally revealed as entirely innocent).
117. *as it were*] Fulgoso's catch-phrase.

Although I saw the winners share my money:
His lordship and an honest gentleman
Pursed it, but not so merrily as I   120
Whistled it off.   *Whistles.*
Piero.   A noble confidence.
Futelli. [*Aside to Guzman*] D'ee note your rival?
Guzman. [*Aside to Futelli*]   With contempt I do.
Fulgoso. I can forgo things nearer than my gold,
    Allied to my affections, and my blood;
    Yea, honour, as it were, with the same kind   125
    Of careless confidence, and come off fairly
    Too, as it were.
Piero.   But not your love, Fulgoso.
Fulgoso. No, she's inherent, and mine own past losing.
Piero. It tickles me to think with how much state
    You, as it were, did run at tilt in love   130
    Before your Amoretta.
Fulgoso.   Broke my lance.
Piero. Of wit, of wit.
Fulgoso.   I mean so, as it were,
    And laid flat on her back both horse and woman.
Piero. Right, as it were.
Fulgoso.   What else, man, as it were.
Guzman. Did you do this to her? Dare you to vaunt   135
    Your triumph, we being present? Um, ha, um.
                    Fulgoso whistles the Spanish Pavane.
Futelli. What think you, don, of this brave man?
Guzman.   A man?
    It is some truss of reeds, or empty cask,
    In which the wind with whistling sports itself.
Futelli. Bear up, sir, he's your rival. Budge not from him 140

121.1.] *Weber; appears in roman in Q, as if part of the text.*   125. kind] *Weber;*
kind. *Q.*   136.1.] *Weber; in Q this appears in the margin beside ll.* 135–7.

---

125. *Yea, honour*] even honour itself.
128. *inherent*] permanently attached.
136.1. *Spanish Pavane*] slow and stately dance. In *'Tis Pity*, Poggio
observes 'I have seen a mule trot the Spanish pavin with a better grace'
(1.2.120–1).
138. *truss*] bundle.
cask] barrel.

An inch; your grounds are honour.
Piero.   Stoutly ventured,
   Don; hold him to't.
Fulgoso.   Protest, a fine conceit,
   A very fine conceit, and thus I told her
   That, for mine own part, if she liked me, so,
   If not, not; 'For, my duck or doe,' said I,   145
   'It is no fault of mine that I am noble;
   Grant it another may be noble too,
   And then we're both one noble; better still.
   Habs-nabs, good, wink and choose.' If one must have her,
   The other goes without her; best of all.   150
   My spirit is too high to fight for woman.
   I am too full of mercy to be angry;
   A foolish generous quality, from which
   No might of man can beat me, I'm resolved.
Guzman. Hast thou a spirit then, ha? Speaks thy weapon   155
   Toledo language, Bilbao, or dull Pisa?
   If an Italian blade, or Spanish metal,
   Be brief. We challenge answer.
Futelli.   Famous don!
Fulgoso. What does he talk? My weapon speaks no language,
   'Tis a Dutch iron truncheon.
Guzman.   Dutch?
Fulgoso.   And if need be,   160
   'Twill maul one's hide, in spite of who says nay.
Guzman. Dutch to a Spaniard? Hold me!
Fulgoso.   Hold me too,

141–2. ventured / Don] *Weber*; ventured, Don *Q.*   149. Habs-nabs] *Q*;
Hab-nab's *Gifford.*

142. *Protest, a fine conceit*] I declare, an excellent idea.
149. *Habs-nabs*] hit or miss.
good] good sir.
wink and choose] close your eyes and take your pick.
156.] Toledo, Bilbao and Pisa were all places where swords were manu-
factured. 'Bilbo' is also found in *The Queen*, a play which is almost certainly
by Ford (3.1), and Vasques in *'Tis Pity She's a Whore* says scornfully, 'Spoon-
meat is a wholesomer diet than a Spanish blade' (1.2.50–1).
160. *Dutch*] The long occupation of the Protestant Netherlands by the
Catholic Spanish had created great ill-feeling between the two nations.
truncheon] short thick staff or club.

Sirrah, if th'art my friend, for I love no fighting;
Yet hold me lest in pity I fly off.
If I must fight, I must; in a scurvy quarrel   165
I defy hes and shes. Twit me with Dutch?
Hang Dutch and French, hang Spanish and Italians,
Christians and Turks! Pew-waw; all's one to me,
I know what's what, I know on which side
My bread is buttered.
Guzman.   Buttered! Dutch again?   170
You come not with intention to affront us?
Fulgoso. Front me no fronts. If thou beest angry, squabble:
Here's my defence, and thy destruction –
                                   Whistles a charge.
If friends, shake hands, and go with me to dinner.
Guzman. We will embrace the motion; it doth relish.   175
The cavaliero treats on terms of honour;
Peace is not to be balked on fair conditions.
Futelli. Still don is don the great.
Piero.   He shows the greatness
Of his vast stomach in the quick embracement
Of th'other's dinner.
Futelli.   'Twas the ready means   180
To catch his friendship.
Piero.   You're a pair of worthies
That make the nine no wonder.
Futelli.   Now since fate
Ordains that one of two must be the man,
The man of men which must enjoy alone

---

169. on which side] *Q*; upon *Gifford.*   173.1.] *Weber; appears in roman in Q,
as if part of the text.*   181. You're] *Weber;* Y'are *Q, Nogami;* Ye're *Gifford.*

164.] Hold on to me just in case I get carried away to pity. It is hard to
see what might move Fulgoso to pity; perhaps the phrase is transferred and
it is Piero, Fulgoso's sponsor, who should take pity on Guzman by preventing
Fulgoso from beating him to a pulp.

168. *Pew-waw*] Rubbish.

170. *Dutch again?*] Guzman makes the association, common at the time,
between butter and the Netherlands.

181–2.] The Nine Worthies consisted of three classical figures, Hector,
Alexander and Julius Caesar, three from the Old Testament, Joshua, David
and Judas Maccabeus, and three Christians, King Arthur, Charlemagne and
the French crusader Godfrey of Bouillon.

Love's darling Amoretta, both take liberty   185
To show himself before her, without cross
Of interruption, one of t'other. He,
Whose sacred mystery of earthly blessings
Crowns the pursuit, be happy.
Piero.   And till then
Live brothers in society.
Guzman.   We are fast.   190
Fulgoso. I vow a match: I'll feast the don today
And fast with him tomorrow.
Guzman.   Fair conditions.

Enter ADURNI, SPINELLA, AMORETTA,
[*and*] CASTANNA.

Adurni. Futelli and Piero, follow speedily.
Piero. My Lord, we wait ye.
Futelli.   We shall soon return.   *Exeunt.*
Fulgoso. What's that? I saw a sound.
Guzman.   A voice for certain.   195
Fulgoso. It named a lord.
Guzman.   Here are lords too, we take it;
We carry blood about us rich and haughty
As any the twelve Caesars.
Fulgoso.   Gulls or moguls,
Tag, rag, or other, hogen mogen van den,

---

199. hogen mogen] *This ed.*; Hoger-Mogen *Q, Weber*; hogen-mogen *Gifford*;
Hogen Mogen *Nogami.*

---

190. *fast*] firmly bonded.
195. *I saw a sound*] Cf. Bottom in *A Midsummer Night's Dream* 4.1.209–10,
'The eye of man hath not heard'.
198. *the twelve Caesars*] Suetonius's *The Lives of the Twelve Caesars* told the
story of the rulers of Rome from Julius Caesar to Domitian.
Gulls or moguls] Fulgoso plays punningly on the name of the Mogul (now
more usually Mughal) rulers of India. When Ford wrote, the throne was
occupied by Shah Jahan (reigned 1628–58), builder of the Taj Mahal. Sir
Thomas Roe, who was a member of the circle of Ford's early dedicatee the
earl of Pembroke, had served as ambassador to Mughal India between 1615
and 1619, during the reign of Jahangir, father of Shah Jahan.
199. *hogen mogen*] version of the Dutch term for 'their high mightinesses',
i.e. the council of the States-General of the United Provinces, and hence by
extension a general term for the Dutch.
van den] Dutch for 'of the', but probably included more to add to the
generally Dutch flavour than for its sense.

Skipjacks, or *chiauses*. Whoo! The brace are flinched;   200
The pair of shavers are sneaked from us, don.
Why, what are we?
Guzman.   The valiant will stand to't.
Fulgoso. So say I; we will eat and drink, and squander,
Till all do split again.
Guzman.   March on with greediness. *Exeunt.*

[ACT 2 SCENE 2]

Enter MARTINO *and* LEVIDOLCE.

Martino. You cannot answer what a general tongue
Objects against your folly! I may curse
The interest you lay claim to in my blood.
Your mother, my dear niece, did die, I thought,
Too soon, but she is happy. Had she lived   5
Till now and known the vanities your life
Hath dealt in, she had wished herself a grave
Before a timely hour.
Levidolce.   Sir, consider
My sex. Were I mankind, my sword should quit
A wounded honour, and reprieve a name   10
From injury, by printing on their bosoms
Some deadly character, whose drunken surfeits
Vomit such base aspersions. As I am,

---

200. *chiauses*] *This ed.*; Chouses *Q*; chiouses *Gifford conj.*   6. vanities your
life] *Weber*; vanities of your life *Q*.

200. *Skipjacks*] Gifford saw this as an attempt at *sanjiak*, a Turkish officer,
by analogy with chiauses, but it is also a standard term for a
whipper-snapper.
chiauses] Turkish messengers.
flinched] sneaked off.
201. *shavers*] swindlers.
204. *do split*] is wrecked (of a ship).
1. *a general tongue*] common talk.

7–8. *she . . . hour*] she would have wished to die before her time. Martino
was sad when Levidolce's mother died, but now perceives her early death
as a blessing, since her daughter's behaviour would have led her to tire of life.
9. *mankind*] male.
quit] pay the debt due to.

Scorn and contempt is virtue; my desert
Stands far above their malice.
Martino.   Levidolce,   15
Hypocrisy puts on a holy robe,
Yet never changeth nature. Call to mind
How in your girl's days you fell, forsooth,
In love, and married – married, hark ye, whom?
A trencher-waiter; shrewd preferment! But   20
Your childhood then excused that fault, for so
Footmen have run away with lusty heirs,
And stable-grooms reached to some fair ones'
     chambers.
Levidolce. Pray let not me be bandied, sir, and baffled
By your intelligence.
Martino.   So, touched to the quick,   25
Fine mistress? I will then rip up at length
The progress of your infancy. In colour
Of disagreement you must be divorced;
Were so, and I must countenance the reasons.
On better hopes I did, nay took you home,   30
Provided you my care, nay justified
Your alteration, joyed to entertain
Such visitants of worth and rank as tendered
Civil respects; but then, even then –
Levidolce.   What then?
Sweet uncle, do not spare me.
Martino.   I more shame   35
To fear my hospitality was bawd,

15–16. Levidolce,   /   Hypocrisy] *Weber;   Levidolche,* hypocrisie   *Q.*
27. infancy] *Q;* infamy *conj. Gifford.*

18. *girl's days*] As always for the Devon-born Ford, the word 'girl' is disyllabic (girrul).
20. *trencher-waiter*] one who carries the plates or wooden boards on which food was served at the table of his patron or master.
shrewd] harmful, injurious.
preferment] advancement.
24. *bandied*] talked about (*OED* v.5).
baffled.] disgraced.
25. *intelligence*] information.
27. *In colour*] on pretence.
29. *Were so*] that duly happened.

And name it so, to your unchaste desires,
Than you to hear and know it.
Levidolce.   Whose whore am I?
For that's your plainest meaning.
Martino.   Were you modest,
The word you uttered last would force a blush.   40
Adurni is a bounteous lord; 'tis said
He parts with gold and jewels like a free
And liberal purchaser; 'a wriggles in
To ladies' pleasures by a right of pension;
But you know none of this. You are grown a tavern-talk,   45
Matter for fiddlers' songs. I toil to build
The credit of my family, and you
To pluck up the foundation! Even this morning,
Before the common council, young Malfato –
Convented for some lands he held, supposed   50
Belonged to certain orphans – as I questioned
His tenure in particulars, he answered,
My worship needed not to flaw his right:
For if the humour held him, he could make
A jointure to my overliving niece,   55
Without oppression; bade me tell her, too,

45.] *Weber; two lines in Q* (this / You).

44. *by a right of pension*] by means of offering payment.
45. *But you know none of this*] Martino sarcastically pretends that this is all news to Levidolce.
48. *foundation*] the base, either natural or artificial, on which a building is erected. Martino thinks of his family, or metaphorical house, as if it were a literal house, which Levidolce is working to undermine.
50. *Convented*] summoned, brought before.
53. *to flaw*] to pick holes in.
55. *jointure*] estate given to a wife intended to support her in her widowhood.
overliving] surviving (*OED* overliving adj., citing this as an example), a sense confirmed by the idea of a jointure. However, the word also suggests *OED*'s over-living as a noun, meaning living in too self-indulgent a manner. Malfato is clearly still smarting from having been propositioned by Levidolce earlier.
56. *Without oppression*] without being tyrannical or using his authority unjustly.

She was a kind young soul, and might in time
Be sued to by a loving man, no doubt.
Here was a jolly breakfast!
Levidolce.   Uncles are privileged
More than our parents; some wise man in state   60
Hath rectified, no doubt, your knowledge, sir.
Whiles all the policy for public business
Was spent, for want of matter, I by chance
Fell into grave discourse! But by your leave,
I from a stranger's table rather wish   65
To earn my bread, than from a friend's by gift
Be daily subject to unfit reproofs.
Martino. Come, come, to the point.
Levidolce.   All the curses
Due to a ravisher of sober truth
Dam up their graceless mouths.
Martino.   Now you turn rampant,   70
Just in the wench's trim and garb. These prayers
    Speak your devotion purely.
Levidolce.   Sir, alas,
What would you have me do? I have no orators
More than my tears to plead my innocence,
Since you forsake me, and are pleased to lend   75
An open ear against my honest fame.
Would all their spite could harry my contents

---

70. Dam up] *Weber*; Dambe up *Q*; Damn up *Nogami*.

---

57. *kind*] generous.
58. *sued to*] courted.
loving man] man in search of a girl.
59. *Here was a jolly breakfast!*] Here was a fine way to start the day!
59–60. *Uncles ... parents*] Ford also depicts close relationships with uncles in *The Fancies Chaste and Noble*, *The Broken Heart* and *The Lover's Melancholy*.
60. *some wise man in state*] someone whose opinion is valued in civic affairs.
61. *rectified ... your knowledge*] put you right on that score.
60–4. *some ... discourse!*] Levidolce suggests that the arbiters of city affairs ran out of serious business to talk about and so fell to discussing her instead.
70. *dam*] Q's 'dambe' has a primary sense of damming or stopping, but also plays on 'damn', picking up the idea of curses.
rampant] wild, out of control.
71. *Just ... garb*] in exactly the usual style of a wanton woman.

Unto a desperate ruin. O dear goodness,
There is a right for wrongs.
Martino.   There is, but first
Sit in commission on your own defects,   80
Accuse yourself, be your own jury, judge
And executioner. I make no sport
Of my vexation.
Levidolce.   All the short remains
Of undesirèd life shall only speak
Th'extremity of penance; your opinion   85
Enjoins it too.
Martino.   Enough; thy tears prevail
Against credulity.
Levidolce.   My miseries,
As in a glass, present me the rent face
Of an unguided youth.

            Enter TRELCATIO [*holding*] *a letter.*

Martino.   No more. – Trelcatio,
Some business speeds you hither?
Trelcatio.   Happy news!   90
Signor Martino, pray, your ear [*Draws him aside.*]:
    my nephew
Auria hath done brave service, and I hear
(Let's be exceeding private) is returned
High in the duke of Florence's respects.
'Tis said – but make no words – that 'a has firked   95
And mumbled the roguy Turks.

---

80. Sit] *Weber; the t is merely a dot in Q.*   89. SD] *This ed.; marginal in Q
between 87 and 89: Enter Trel-/catio. A let-/ter.*   96. have] *Gifford;* know *Q.*

80. *Sit in commission*] act as judge with power to decide.
82–3. *I make no sport / Of*] I take no amusement in, I don't make a joke of.
88. *glass*] mirror.
    rent] torn. In classical literature distraught or griefstricken women tear
their faces with their nails.
93. *private*] undisturbed, i.e. safe from being overheard.
95. *firked*] trounced (also found in this sense in *The Lover's Melancholy*
4.2.434, 'I will firk his trangdido'); also implies driving people out. In *The
Rogue*, Guzman de Alfarache's uncle is pleased that he 'firkt' the 'young
Rogue' he supposes has tried to trick him (Alemán 3, p. 355).
96. *mumbled*] roughly handled, knocked about (also found in this sense
in *The Lover's Melancholy* 5.1.132, 'He has mumbled his nose, that 'tis as big
as a great codpiece'). Auria has comprehensively beaten the Turks.
    roguy] disreputable, rascally.

Martino.   Why would you have
        His merits so unknown?
Trelcatio.   I am not yet
        Confirmed at full. Withdraw, and you shall read
        All what this paper talks.
Martino.   So; Levidolce,
        You know our mind; be cheerful. Come, Trelcatio.   100
        Causes of joy or grief do seldom happen
        Without companions near; thy resolutions
        Have given another birth to my contents.
                    Ex[eunt MARTINO *and* TRELCATIO].
Levidolce. Even so, wise uncle, much good do ye. Discovered!
        I could fly out, mix vengeance with my love.   105
        Unworthy man, Malfato! My good lord,
        My hot-in-blood rare lord, grows cold too! Well,
        Rise, dotage, into rage, and sleep no longer;
        Affection turned to hatred threatens mischief.
                                               Exit.

                        [ACT 2 SCENE 3]

        Enter PIERO, AMORETTA, FUTELLI *and* CASTANNA.

Piero. In the next gallery you may behold
        Such living pictures, lady, such rich pieces
        Of kings, and queens, and princes that you'd think
        They breathe and smile upon ye.

99–100. Levidolce, / You] *Weber*; Levidolche, you *Q.*   102. companions
near; thy] *Weber (subst.)*; companions, neere thy *Q.*   103.1. SD] *Weber
(subst.); Exit Q.*   107. cold] *Weber*; could *Q.*

        have] Q's 'know' is presumably an error prompted by 'unknowne' in the
line below. Gifford's suggestion of 'have' makes good sense of the line.
        108. *dotage*] excessive love.

Amoretta.   Ha' they crownths,
    Great crownths oth gold upon their headths?
Piero.   Pure gold,   5
    Drawn all in state.
Amoretta.   How many horthes, pray,
    Are ith their chariots?
Piero.   Sixteen, some twenty.
Castanna. My sister! Wherefore left we her alone?
    Where stays she, gentlemen?
Futelli.   Viewing the rooms;
    'Tis like you'll meet her in the gallery.   10
    This house is full of curiosities
    Most fit for ladies' sights.
Amoretta.   Yeth, yeth, the thight
    Of printhes ith a fine thight.
Castanna.   Good, let us find her.
Piero. Sweet ladies, this way. [*Aside*] See the doors sure.
Futelli.   [*Aside*] Doubt not.
                                        Ex[eunt].

---

13. printhes] *This ed.*; printhethes *Q.*   14. SD] *Weber; Exit Q.*

4.] Amoretta's lisp is a source of comedy but also serves to sexualise her, since lisping proves to be associated with kissing. This invites us to read her, Levidolce, and Spinella as part of Ford's typical trilogy of women of different degrees of emotional authenticity (see McMaster).

10. *gallery*] Although we cannot be sure about the interior layout of the Phoenix (Wickham 623–5), it is clear that it had an upper stage (Stevens 495), of which Ford also makes use in *'Tis Pity She's a Whore* when Annabella appears on it. Compare too *Women Beware Women*, in which Bianca is told she is going to behold works of art but is in fact raped by the Duke.

11. *curiosities*] strange and interesting objects. Many Renaissance dignitaries had curiosity cabinets in which they displayed collections of oddities and rarities. Curiosity, with a general meaning of (over-) scrupulousness, is a recurrent word in the play; cf 5.2.177, where Aurelio attributes his intervention to 'A rash and over-busy curiosity'.

12. *Most fit for ladies' sights*] Tilley records 'Dear bought and far fetched are dainties for ladies', and variations on this, as proverbial in the period (Tilley 138, D12).

13. *printhes*] Q's *printhethes* makes nonsense of both the metre and the sense, since Amoretta's thoughts are firmly fixed on princes. Perhaps the compositor was distracted by the distortion to the words caused by Amoretta's lisp.

[ACT 2 SCENE 4]

Enter ADURNI *and* SPINELLA.

SONG.

Pleasures, beauty, youth attend ye
Whiles the spring of nature lasteth.
Love and melting thoughts attend ye;
Use the time, ere winter hasteth.
Active blood, and free delight,   5
Place and privacy invite.
Do, do! Be kind as fair,
Lose not opportunity for air.
She is cruel that denies it,
Bounty best appears in granting,   10
Stealth of sport as soon supplies it,
Whiles the dues of love are wanting.
Here's the sweet exchange of bliss,

0.1 SD] *This ed.; SONG precedes the entrance in Q, and the whole song is in italics.*   3. attend] *Q*; befriend *conj Gifford.*

1–16.] William Lawes's setting for the song, with slightly altered wording, survives in BM. ADD. MS. 31432 (see Nogami, Appendix C, and Ian Spink, *Musica Britannica*, 33 (1971), p. 133). Every aspect of the song, which is presumably sung by a servant of Adurni's or by someone employed by him for the occasion, is designed to encourage Spinella to yield to Adurni's desires. The spring/winter references evoke a classic 'carpe diem' theme (cf. Herrick's 'Gather ye rosebuds while ye may'). If its placement at the head of the scene indicates that it functions instead of the music usually played between acts or scenes to allow for the retrimming of the candles, then it is perhaps sung while the actors take up their positions for the next scene.

    3. *melting*] sexually yielding.

    4. *Use the time*] seize the opportunity.

    5. *Active*] ready and able for sex.

    6. *Place and privacy invite*] Opportunity is offered by the conveniently empty room.

    7. *Do, do!*] Have sex! 'To do the deed' is a standard euphemism for having intercourse.

    kind] yielding, giving; also cf. Malfato's insulting characterisation of Levidolce, who has propositioned him, as a 'kind young soul' (2.2.57).

    8. *air*] Perhaps in the sense of freedom.

    11. *sport*] sexual activity.

When each whisper proves a kiss.
In the game are felt no pains,   15
For in all the loser gains.

Adurni. Plead not, fair creature, without sense of pity
So incompassionately 'gainst a service
In nothing faulty more than pure obedience.
My honours and my fortunes are led captives   20
In triumph by your all-commanding beauty,
And if you ever felt the power of love,
The rigour of an uncontrollèd passion,
The tyranny of thoughts, consider mine,
In some proportion, by the strength of yours.   25
Thus may you yield and conquer.
Spinella.   Do not study,
My lord, to apparel folly in the stead
Of costly colours. Henceforth cast off far,
Far from your noblest nature the contempt
Of goodness, and be gentler to your fame   30
By purchase of a life to grace your story.
Adurni. Dear, how sweetly
Reproof drops from that balmy spring, your breath!
Now could I read a lecture of my griefs,
Unearth a mine of jewels at your foot,   35
Command a golden shower to rain down,
Impoverish every kingdom of the east
Which traffics richest clothes and silks, would you
Vouchsafe one unspleened chiding to my riot;

---

27. stead] *Weber*; steed *Q*; weed *conj. Gifford.*   33. drops] *Weber*; droopes *Q*.

15. *game*] sexual act.
16.] Unlike gambling, at which Spinella has lost money, this is a 'game' at which no one loses.
27. *stead*] use or advantage (*OED* 13). Weber conjectured that Ford might mean it as a substantive form of 'to bestead'.
27–8. *to ... colours*] to dress up foolish behaviour in a showy disguise.
32.] A half line.
36. *golden shower*] In Greek mythology, Danaë, the mother of Perseus, conceived when Zeus rained down on her in the form of a golden shower.
38. *silks*] Marco Polo, famous for travelling along the Silk Road to Cathay, was imprisoned in Genoa on his return and wrote the account of his journey there. This is therefore an appropriate offer for a Genoese to make.
39. *unspleened*] mild, temperate.

Else such a sacrifice can but beget   40
Suspicion of returns to my devotion
In mercenary blessings, for that saint
To whom I vow myself must never want
Fit offerings to her altar.
Spinella.   Auria, Auria,
Fight not for name abroad, but come, my husband,   45
Fight for thy wife at home!
Adurni.   Oh, never rank,
Dear cruelty, one that is sworn your creature
Amongst your country's enemies. I use
No force, but humble words, delivered from
A tongue that's secretary to my heart.   50
Spinella. How poorly some, tame to their wild desires,
Fawn on abuse of virtue! Pray, my lord,
Make not your house my prison.
Adurni.   Grant a freedom
To him who is the bondman to your beauty.

                                        A noise within.

          Enter AURELIO, CASTANNA, AMORETTA, FUTELLI
                         and PIERO.

Aurelio. Keep back, ye close contrivers of false pleasures,   55
Or I shall force ye back! Can it be possible?
Locked up, and singly too? Chaste hospitality!
A banquet in a bed-chamber! Adurni,
Dishonourable man!

---

46. rank] *Weber*; canke *Q.*   54.1. *A noise within*] *Weber; in Q this SD appears in the margin next to ll.* 53–4 *as: A noise* / *within.*

---

40. *sacrifice*] act of worship. Adurni simultaneously speaks of Spinella as if she were a saint at whose altar he will lay offerings and as if she were to be bought. 'Sacrifice', a favourite Ford word, always has erotic overtones, as in the title of his tragedy *Love's Sacrifice*. Adurni deploys a number of terms and ideas familiar enough from love poetry, casting his 'mistress' as a goddess or saint and himself as a worshipper at her altar, but Spinella's love for her husband and horror at his avowals makes such language ring even more emptily than usual.

43. *want*] lack.

47. *your creature*] one who owes everything to you.

50. *secretary*] confidant or secret-keeper. Cf. *The Fancies Chaste and Noble* 5.2.34–5, 'You will finde his tongue / But a just Secretary to his heart'.

57. *singly*] alone.

Adurni.   What sees this rudeness
That can broach scandal here?
Aurelio.   [*To Adurni*] For you hereafter.   60
[*To Spinella*] O woman, lost to every brave report,
Thy wrongèd Auria is come home with glory;
Prepare a welcome to uncrown the greatness
Of his prevailing fates.
Spinella.   Whiles you, belike,
Are furnished with some news for entertainment   65
Which must become your friendship, to be knit
More fast betwixt your souls by my removal
Both from his heart and memory.
Adurni.   Rich conquest,
To triumph on a lady's injured fame
Without a proof or warrant.
Futelli.   Have I life, sir?   70
Faith, Christianity?
Piero.   Put me on the rack,
The wheel, or the galleys, if –
Aurelio.   Peace, factors
In merchandise of scorn! Your sounds are deadly.
Castanna, I could pity your consent
To such ignoble practice, but I find   75
Coarse fortunes easily seduced, and herein
All claim to goodness ceases.
Castanna.   Use your tyranny.
Spinella. What rests behind for me? Out with it.
Aurelio.   Horror
Becoming such a forfeit of obedience.

---

61. *brave*] good (*OED* a., n.3).

72. *factors*] agents, traders. Since 'fact' can mean crime, 'factors' could also evoke the idea of 'malefactors'.

74–5. *Castanna . . . practice*] The fact that Aurelio had expected Castanna to behave better suggests a possible interest in her and thus invites a comparison with Romanello in *The Fancies Chaste and Noble*, who loses Castamela to another man after casting unjust aspersions on her behaviour. Similarly, Aurelio might have seemed a possible partner for Castanna before her surprise betrothal to Adurni.

78. *Horror*] Glossed as 'fearefull sorrow' by Edmund Coote in *The English School-master* in 1596. Aurelio threatens Spinella with suffering in proportion to what he takes her crime to be.

Hope not that any falsity in friendship   80
Can palliate a broken faith; it dares not.
Leave in thy prayers, fair vow-breaking wanton,
To dress thy soul new, whose purer whiteness
Is sullied by thy change from truth to folly.
A fearful storm is hovering; it will fall.   85
No shelter can avoid it. Let the guilty
Sink under their own ruin.   *Exit.*
Spinella.   How unmanly
His anger threatens mischief!
Amoretta.   Whom, I prithee,
Doth the man speak to?
Adurni. [*To Spinella*]   Lady, be not moved;
I will stand champion for your honour, hazard   90
All what is dearest to me.
Spinella.   Mercy, heaven!
Champion for me, and Auria living? Auria!
He lives, and for my guard my innocence,
As free as are my husband's clearest thoughts,
Shall keep off vain constructions. I must beg   95
Your charities: sweet sister, yours to leave me –
I need no fellows now. Let me appear,
Or mine own lawyer, or in open court
(Like some forsaken client) in my suit
Be cast for want of honest plea. Oh, misery!   *Exit.* 100
Adurni. Her resolution's violent. Quickly, follow!

---

83. new] *Q*; [a]new *Gifford.*   97. fellows] *Q*; followers *Gifford.*

81. *palliate*] alleviate, lessen.
85–7. *A fearful . . . ruin*] Aurelio's conviction that everyone is doomed and will suffer appropriately may recall the Friar in *'Tis Pity She's a Whore*, who tells Giovanni 'I leave thee to despair' (5.3.69).
93–5.] Spinella is confident that Auria's generous, trusting nature will show him her innocence and not be misled by false interpretations of her behaviour.
97. *fellows*] companions.
97–100.] Either I will plead my own cause by myself or, if I were to make the matter more public, let my arguments, like those of someone whose patron has deserted him, fail because of the dishonour attached to the pleader. Spinella will rely entirely on a private appeal to Auria.

Castanna. By no means, sir; y'ave followed her already,
    I fear with too much ill success in trial
    Of unbecoming courtesies, your welcome
    Ends in so sad a farewell.
Adurni.   I will stand   105
    The roughness of th'encounter like a gentleman,
    And wait ye to your homes, whate'er befall me.
                                               Exeunt.

103–5. *fear … farewell*] I am afraid that your attempt at inopportune gallantry has produced a very bad outcome. Castanna assumes that the disastrous conclusion to the visit can only mean that Adurni has been pestering Spinella with unwanted and unfitting attentions.

107. *wait ye*] escort you. Adurni's concept of being a gentleman is apparently limited to formalities.

Act 3

Enter FULGOSO *and* GUZMAN.

Fulgoso. I say, don, brother mine, win her and wear her,
 And so will I; if't be my luck to lose her,
 I lose a pretty wench, and there's the worst on't.
Guzman. 'Wench' said ye, most mechanically? Faugh!
 'Wench' is your trull, your blowse, your dowdy; but, 5
 Sir brother, he who names my queen of love
 Without his bonnet vailed, or saying grace,
 As at some paranymphal feast, is rude,
 Nor versed in literature. Dame Amoretta,
 Lo, I am sworn thy champion!
Fulgoso.   So am I too; 10
 Can as occasion serves, if she turn scurvy,
 Unswear myself again, and ne'er change colours.
 Pish, man, the best – though call 'em ladies, madams,
 Fairs, fines and honeys – are but flesh and blood,
 And now and then too, when the fit's come on 'em, 15
 Will prove themselves but flirts, and tirlery puffkins.

ACT 3 [SCENE I].] *This ed.; Actus Tertius. Q.* 9. Nor] *Q*; Not *Gifford.*

1. *win her and wear her*] proverbial.
5. *trull*] cheap prostitute.
 blowse] beggar's wench.
 dowdy] shabbily dressed woman.
7. *bonnet vailed*] hat removed in sign of respect.
8. *paranymphal*] *OED*, giving this as the only usage, conjectures 'nuptial' (from 'paranymph', meaning bridesmaid or wedding attendant).
12. *ne'er change colours*] not alter my allegiance; also with a suggestion of not needing to blush for his actions.
16. *tirlery*] flighty, trifling.
 puffkins] *OED*, citing this as the only known usage, suggests flighty or capricious persons. However see also *OED* puff n.,a. 1d, a small quantity of smoke or vapour, of which puffkins would form a credible diminutive. It might also be derived from the puffball mushroom, which breaks up into a cloud of spores, since a mushroom was a common image for a social climber or upstart.

Guzman. Our choler must advance.

Fulgoso.   Dost long for a beating?
    Shall's try a slash? Here's that shall do't! [*Draws his*
        sword.] I'll tap
    A gallon of thy brains, and fill thy hogshead
    With two of wine for't.

Guzman.   Not in friendship, brother.   20

Fulgoso. Or whistle thee into an ague; hang't,
    Be sociable: drink till we roar and scratch,
    Then drink ourselves asleep again. The fashion!
    Thou dost not know the fashion.

Guzman.   Her fair eyes,
    Like to a pair of pointed beams drawn from   25
    The sun's most glorious orb, does dazzle sight,
    Audacious to gaze there; then over those
    A several bow of jet securely twines
    In semicircles; under them two banks
    Of roses red and white, divided by   30
    An arch of polished ivory, surveying
    A temple from whence oracles proceed,
    More gracious than Apollo's, more desired
    Than amorous songs of poets softly tuned.

Fulgoso. Hey-day, what's this?

Guzman.   Oh, but those other parts,   35
    All –

Fulgoso. All? Hold there, I bar play under board;
    My part yet lies therein; you never saw

---

26. does dazzle] *Q*; do dazzle *Weber*.   35–6. parts, / All] *Weber*; parts, all *Q*.

---

17. *Our choler must advance*] I am so angry I must have headway.

18. *Shall's*] shall we. Perhaps another of Ford's Devonshire forms.

that] his sword, which he presumably touches or indicates.

21. *whistle thee into an ague*] drive you into a fever by whistling.

24–34.] a blazon – that is, a catalogue of a woman's beauties, common in poetry of the period.

28. *several bow of jet*] two dark eyebrows.

29–30. *banks / Of roses*] Amoretta's cheeks.

31. *An arch of polished ivory*] Her nose.

32.] Her mouth.

36. *play under board*] play under the table or playing surface; metaphorically directing the gaze towards Amoretta's lower body.

37. *My part yet lies therein*] The lewd punning plays on 'part' as penis and what it might be penetrating.

The things you wire-draw thus.
Guzman.   I have dreamt
Of every part about her, can lay open
Her several inches as exactly – mark it –   40
As if I had took measure with a compass,
A rule, or yard, from head to foot.
Fulgoso.   Oh, rare,
And all this in a dream?
Guzman.   A very dream.
Fulgoso. My waking brother soldier is turned
Into a sleeping carpenter or tailor,   45

Enter BENAZZI *as an outlaw.* LEVIDOLCE *above.*

Which goes for half a man – what's he? Bear up!
Benazzi. Death of reputation, the wheel, strappado, galleys,
rack are ridiculous fopperies: goblins to fright babies.

---

38. I] *Q*; [But] I *Gifford.*   45.1.] *This ed.; in Q the SD takes* 4 *lines to fit in margin: Enter Benat-/zi as an out-law. Levi-/doche above.*   47–51.] *Weber; verse in Q.*

---

38. *wire-draw*] Usually sketch, but the phrase can also mean to spin out or strain an argument farther than it should properly go, which seems to be the gist of Fulgoso's complaint against Guzman.

39–40. *lay open / Her several inches*] Officially, Guzman seems to suggest he could describe her height, but the idea of revealing her vagina is also implied.

42. *yard*] yardstick, but also a term for the penis.

45.1.] Levidolce's literal elevation here proves the preparative to a moral restoration. Cf. Annabella in *'Tis Pity She's a Whore*, who is first seen above (1.2.31), descends after her first sight of her brother (1.2.144), and then returns to the balcony to make her peace with the Friar and persuade him to carry her letter of repentance to Giovanni (5.1.0).

44-5.] Fulgoso comments on the unmilitary notion of Guzman taking mensurements.

47. *Death of reputation*] Loss of a general good opinion. In this respect, as in so many others, like *Othello*, where Cassio bemoans the loss of his reputation as fatal (2.2.256–61), *The Lady's Trial* is always aware that what matters is not only what *has* happened, but what is generally thought to have happened.

47–8. *the wheel, strappado, galleys, rack*] All forms of Renaissance punishment involving physical torture. Criminals could be bound to a wheel which was rolled until their bodies were broken; have their hands tied to a pulley behind their back which was then used to suspend them in mid-air and drop them abruptly (the strappado); be sent to row in the galleys; or have their limbs stretched on the rack.

Poor lean-souled rogues, they will swoon at the scar of a
pin; one tear dropped from their harlots' eyes breeds   50
earthquakes in their bones.

Fulgoso. Bless us, a monster patched of dagger-bombast,
His eyes like copper basins; 'a has changed
Hair with a shag-dog.

Guzman.   Let us then avoid him,
Or stand upon our guard; the foe approaches.   55

Benazzi. Cut-throats by the score abroad, come home, and
rot in fripperies; brave man at arms, go, turn pander, do;
stalk for a mess of warm broth – damnable! Honourable
cuts are but badges for a fool to vaunt; the raw-ribbed
apothecary poisons *cum privilegio*, and is paid. Oh, the   60
commonwealth of beasts is most politicly ordered.

Guzman. Brother, we'll keep aloof; there is no valour
In tugging with a man-fiend.

Fulgoso.   I defy him.
It gabbles like I know not what; believe it,
The fellow's a shrewd fellow at a pink.   65

---

57. rot] *Q*; riot *conj. Weber.*

---

49. *Poor lean-souled rogues*] Benazzi is contemptuous of the kind of man
who could be frightened by the instruments of torture he has just listed.

50–1.] All it takes is for their whores to shed one tear and they tremble
violently.

52. *patched of dagger-bombast*] held together by padding made from
daggers. Fulgoso neatly comines a commnent on Benazzi's shabby clothes
with the implication that he is prone to violence.

53. *His eyes like copper basins*] Like large copper apron sinks, Benazzi's eyes
are big and hollow, because he is hungry, and have a reddish glow.

54. *shag-dog*] dog with shaggy hair.

57. *pander*] pimp.

58. *mess*] portion of food.

59. *raw-ribbed*] having no flesh on his ribs. Ford may be remembering the
apothecary in *Romeo and Juliet*, a play which greatly influenced *'Tis Pity She's
a Whore*, who is so poor that 'Sharp misery had worn him to the bones'
(5.1.41) and is therefore willing to sell Romeo a poison.

60. cum privilegio] Latin for 'with privilege', i.e. 'by right'.

61. *politicly*] judiciously, expediently.

65. *pink*] stab.

Benazzi. Look else; the lion roars, and the spaniel fawns.
Down, cur! The badger bribes the unicorn, that a jury
may not pass upon his pillage. Here the bear fees the
wolf, for he will not howl gratis (beasts call pleading
howling). So then, there the horse complains of the ape's   70
rank-riding; the jockey makes mouths, but is fined for it;
the stag is not jeered by the monkey for his horns; the
ass by the hare for his burden, the ox by the leopard for

66.] *Q; prose Weber, Gifford, Nogami, Keltie.*

66–78.] Benazzi's patter may seem to owe something to the typical comic
bluster of the fake soldier in Renaissance drama, except that, as we later
discover (5.2.207–9), Benazzi has in fact fought valiantly.

67. *The badger bribes the unicorn*] The badger is a weak animal, ill-equipped
for combat; the unicorn is not only armed with a horn but appears as a
supporter in the royal coat of arms, so the phrase suggests corruption at high
levels.

68–70. *Here . . . howling*] Following on from his reference to a jury, Benazzi
seems to be still thinking in legal terms: the bear, a strong but simple animal
which is associated with being baited or muzzled, has to pay the wolf, a more
cunning one, to plead his case in court, since lawyers will do nothing without
payment.

71. *rank-riding*] wild, impetuous riding.
jockey] one who manages horses.
makes mouths] makes faces. Again the idea seems to be one of miscarriage
of justice: one animal complains that another has ridden him badly, but it is
the human in charge of the horse who, despite his protests, is penalised.

72–8. *the stag . . . feet*] The underlying idea here seems to be one of power
structures versus the 'natural order'. The monkey does not make fun of the
stag even though the stag bears horns, the sign of a cuckold, because the
stag is bigger than the monkey and could put those antlers to aggressive use.
The hare similarly steels clear of the bigger donkey, the leopard of the bigger
ox, and the ram of the more aggressive goat, all of which offer instances of
an animal which might be considered to have a natural advantage (speed in
the cases of hare and leopard, while the metaphor of the sheep and the goats
cast the sheep as the saved and the goats as the damned) being bested by
one which does not. Only the fox, epitome of cunning, is able to keep himself
warm in the fur of the beaver, order other animals around and mock everyone with impunity, and is even able to go to sleep in the presence of the lion,
who despite his status as king of beasts is powerless. As a returning soldier,
Benazzi clearly feels that courage counts for nothing in a corrupt civil society
in which cunning alone triumphs. This speech seems to recall Talbot's lament
in *Henry VI*, Part One, 1.5.25–32 that Englishmen, once called dogs because
of their fierceness, now run away like whelps, which mentions oxen running
from leopards as treacherous.

his yoke, nor the goat by the ram for his beard; only the
fox wraps himself warm in beaver, bids the cat mouse,   75
the elephant toil, the boar gather acorns, whiles he grins,
feeds fat, tells tales, laughs at all, and sleeps safe at the
lion's feet. – Save ye, people.

Fulgoso. Why, save thee too, if thou beest of heaven's making.
What art? – Fear nothing, don. We have our blades,   80
Are metal men ourselves, try us who dare.

Guzman. Our brother speaks our mind, think what you please
on't.

Benazzi. A match! Observe well this switch: with this only
switch have I pashed out the brains of thirteen Turks to
the dozen for a breakfast.   85

Fulgoso. What, man? Thirteen? Is't possible thou liest not?

Benazzi. I was once a scholar, then I begged without pity.
From thence I practised law; there a scruple of conscience popped me over the bar. A soldier I turned a
while, but could not procure the letter of preferment.   90
Merchant I would be, and a glut of land-rats gnawed me
to the bones; would have bought an office, but the places
with reversions were catched up; offered to pass into the
court, and wanted trust for clothes; was lastly, for my

---

84. thirteen] *Weber*; tirteen Q.   92. bones] *Weber*; bores Q.

78.*Save ye*] God save ye.
84. *switch*] riding-whip.
pashed] dashed.
83–5. *with . . . breakfast*] Benazzi's supposed feat may recall Prince Hal's
parody of Hotspur, who he imagines 'kills me some six or seven dozens of
Scots at a breakfast' and later announces that he has slain fourteen that day
(1 *Henry IV* 2.4.101–6).
87. *without pity*] without anybody taking pity on me.
87–98.] Benazzi's account of himself recalls that of Edgar in his disguise
as Poor Tom (*King Lear* 3.4.82–94).
89. *popped me over the bar*] expelled me from the society of lawyers.
90. *letter of preferment*] letter of recommendation or promotion.
91. *land-rats*] land-dwelling rats; used as a term of abuse. In *The Merchant
of Venice*, Shylock muses that 'there be land rats and water rats, water thieves
and land thieves, I mean pirates' (1.3.22–3).
92. *bought an office*] purchased an official position.
93. *reversions*] guarantees of succeeding to an office when the present
incumbent leaves it.
94. *trust*] credit.

good parts, pressed into the galleys, took prisoner,   95
redeemed amongst other slaves by your gay great man
– they call him Auria – and am now I know not who,
where or what. How d'ee like me? Say.

Fulgoso. A shaver of all trades; what course of life
Dost mean to follow next? Ha? Speak thy mind.   100

Guzman. Nor be thou daunted, fellow: we ourselves
Have felt the frowns of fortune in our days.

Benazzi. I want extremely, exceedingly, hideously.
                              [*Levidolce*] *throws a purse.*

Levidolce. Take that, enjoy it freely, wisely use
Th'advantage of thy fate, and know the giver.   *Exit.* 105

Fulgoso. Hoy da, a purse in troth! Who dropped't? Stay, stay.
Humph! Have we gypsies here? Oh, mine is safe.
Is't your purse, brother don?

Guzman.   Not mine; I seldom
Wear such unfashionable trash about me.

Fulgoso. Has't any money in it, honest blade?   110
A bots on empty purses!

Guzman.   We defy them.

Benazzi. Stand from about me, as you are mortal! You are
dull clod-pated lumps of mire and garbage. This is the
land of fairies! Imperial queen of elves, I do crouch to
thee [*he bows*], vow my services, my blood, my sinews to   115
thee, sweet sovereign of largesse and liberality. A French

103.1.] *This ed.; in Q appears in the margin beside l. 90.* 104–5. use /
Th'advantage] *This ed.*; use it. / Th'advantage *Q*; use it, / Th'advantage
Weber; use it [to] / Th'advantage *Gifford*; use it / T'advantage
Nogami. 106. dropped't] *This ed.*; dropt *Q.*

95. *pressed*] forcibly enlisted as an oarsman.
99. *shaver*] chap, fellow.
107.] Fulgoso worries that gypsies, notorious for thieving, might be in the
vicinity, so checks his own purse but finds it safe.
109. *unfashionable trash*] something so useless and trivial.
111. *bots*] parasitical worm. 'A bots on' is an expression of execration, not
uncommon in writing of the period.
116. *largesse and liberality*] generosity and open-handedness.
116–19.] Benazzi names the attribute for which each nation was
most famous, e.g. noting that Venice was famous for its courtesans,
before ironically concluding that the English are best at pimping. The
implication is that Levidolce's bounty will enable him to afford the best
of everything.

tailor, neat! Persian cook, dainty! Greek wines, rich!
Flanders mares, stately! Spanish salads, poignant!
Venetian wanton, ravishing! English bawd, unmatchable!
Sirs, I am fitted.   120
Fulgoso. All these thy followers? Miserable pygmies!
Prate sense and don't be mad. I like thy humour,
'Tis pretty odd, and so, as one might say,
I care not greatly if I entertain thee.
Dost want a master? If thou dost I am for thee;   125
Else choose, and snick up. Pish, I scorn to flinch, man.
Guzman. Forsake not fair advancement; money certes
Will fleet and drop off, like a cozening friend.
Who holds it holds a slippery eel by th'tail,
Unless he grip it fast; be ruled by counsel.   130
Benazzi. Excellent. What place shall I be admitted to?
Chamber, wardrobe, cellar, or stable?
Futelli. Why, one and all. Th'art welcome; let's shake hands
on't.
Thy name?

---

126. snick up] *Nogami*; sneake up *Q*; sneck up *Gifford*.   128. fleet] *Q;*
Gifford printed flit, *but Dyce restored it to* fleet.   131–2. to? Chamber] *Weber*;
to? / Chamber *Q*.

---

120. *fitted*] suited, fully equipped.
121. *Miserable pygmies!*] pathetic, insignificant things!.
124. *entertain thee*] give you employment. Fulgoso's attitude recalls that
of Sogliardo when he hires Shift in Act 3 of Jonson's *Every Man Out of His
Humour*.
126. *snick up*] go hang yourself (see *OED* 'snick' v.1 and *N&Q* 30 (25
May 1850): 492–3).
flinch] back off. This, and the fact that Guzman apparently feels obliged
to advise Benazzi to accept, suggest that Benazzi's initial response to the offer
is unenthusiastic and perhaps even aggressive.
127. *certes*] certainly.
128. *fleet*] fade away, dissolve.
cozening] cheating.
131. *place*] position, post.
132. *Chamber, wardrobe, cellar or stable?*] Attendance on Fulgoso's
person, his clothes, his wine or his horses are the possibilities which Benazzi
envisages, apparently assuming that Fulgoso has a larger and grander house-
hold than is in fact the case.

Benazzi.   Parado, sir.

Fulgoso.   The great affairs
    I shall employ thee most in will be news,   135
    And telling what's o'clock, for aught I know yet.

Benazzi. It is, sir, to speak punctually, some hour and half
    eight three thirds of two seconds of one minute over at
    most, sir.

Fulgoso. I do not ask thee now, or if I did   140
    We are not much the wiser; and for news –

Benazzi. Auria the fortunate is this day to be received with
    great solemnity at the city council house; the streets are
    already thronged with lookers-on.

Fulgoso. That's well remembered; brother don, let's trudge,   145
    Or we shall come too late.

Guzman.   By no means, brother.

Fulgoso. Wait close, my ragged new-come.

Benazzi.   As your shadows.

                                        Exeunt.

[ACT 3 SCENE 2]

Enter AURIA, ADURNI, MARTINO, TRELCATIO, AURELIO,
            PIERO *and* FUTELLI.

Auria. Your favours, with these honours, speak your
        bounties,
    And though the low deserts of my success
    Appear in your constructions fair and goodly,

137–9.] *Weber*; half / Eight *Q.*   147. shadows] *Q*; shadow *conj. Dyce*; shadow's *Nogami.*

─────────────────────────────────────

134.] As Benazzi moves back into society, so he begins gradually to speak
its language, verse.

Parado] Parade ground, but also meaning ostentation or display. Benazzi
presumably alludes both to his military background and to the fact that he
is not what he seems. It may also be pertinent that the conquistador Nuño
Beltrán de Guzmán had a close associate named Alonso de Parada.

135. *news*] gathering gossip and information.

145. *trudge*] go, depart.

147. *Wait close*] attend me diligently by being at hand.

new-come] new arrival, novice.

1. *Your favours*] your collective countenancing of me and its manifesta-
tions. 'Your favours' is what the Prologue had requested of the audience.

3. *constructions*] interpretations of events.

Yet I attribute to a noble cause,
Not my abilities, the thanks due to them: 5
The duke of Florence hath too highly prized
My duty in my service, by example
Rather to cherish and encourage virtue
In spirits of action than to crown the issue
Of feeble undertakings. Whiles my life   10
Can stand in use I shall no longer rate it
In value than it stirs to pay that debt
I owe my country for my birth and fortunes.
Martino. Which to make good, our state of Genoa,
Not willing that a native of her own,   15
So able for her safety, should take pension
From any other prince, hath cast upon you
The government of Corsica.
Trelcatio.   Adds thereto,
Besides th'allowance yearly due, for ever
To you and to your heirs the full revenue   20
Belonging to Savona, with the office
Of Admiral of Genoa.
Adurni.   Presenting
By my hands, from their public treasury,
A thousand ducats.
Martino.   But they limit only
One month of stay for your dispatch, no more.   25

4–7. *Yet . . . service*] However, I attribute the thanks you give me not to my
own abilities but to a noble cause, which was the duke of Florence's over-
valuing of what I did in the course of my duty.

7–10. *by example . . . undertakings*] which he did in order to encourage the
eager to acts of prowess rather than to make much of my own not very
meritorious achievements.

10. *Whiles*] as long as.

11. *rate*] value, prize.

18.] Cf. *Othello*, where the successful general is sent from Venice to
Cyprus.

21. *Savona*] city on the west coast of Italy, not far from Genoa, and
famous as the home of Christopher Columbus.

24. *ducats*] gold coins of varying value, used in many European
countries.

25. *dispatch*] departure.

Futelli. In all your great attempts, may you grow thrifty,
    Secure, and prosperous.
Piero.   If you please to rank
    Amongst the humblest one that shall attend
    Instructions under your command, I am
    Ready to wait the charge.
Auria.   Oh, still the state   30
    Engageth me her creature, with the burden
    Unequal for my weakeness. To you, gentlemen,
    I will prove friendly honest, of all mindful.
Adurni. In memory, my lord (such is your style now),
    Of your late fortunate exploits, the council   35
    Amongst their general acts have registered
    The great duke's letters, witness of your merit,
    To stand in characters upon record.
Auria. Load upon load! Let not my want of modesty
    Trespass against good manners; I must study   40
    Retirement to compose this weighty business
    And moderately digest so large a plenty,
    For fear it swell unto a surfeit.
Adurni.   May I
    Be bold to press a visit?
Auria.   At your pleasure;
    Good time of day, and peace.
Omnes.   Health to your lordship.   45
             [*Exeunt all but Adurni and Futelli.*]

---

42. digest] *Weber;* disgest *Q.* 45. SD *Exeunt all but . . .*] *Weber; not in Q.*

---

30. *charge*] command.
34. *style*] title.
38. *characters*] letters of the alphabet.
41. *Retirement*] solitude, removal from company.
42. *digest*] Q's 'disgest' is probably synonymous with 'digest' but Spencer in his edition of *The Broken Heart* retained 'disgestion' (III.ii.61) on the grounds that the other four occurrences of digest/ed/ing in the play lacked the s and that this seemed therefore to be a genuine variant, presumably with a possibility of 'dis' connoting the prefix 'dys', as in 'dystopia'. That would not, however, apply here.
43. *surfeit*] excessive eating and the illness that can arise therefrom.
45. Omnes] All.

Adurni. What of Spinella yet?

Futelli.   Quite lost; no prints,
 Or any tongue of tracing her. However
 Matters are huddled up, I doubt my lord
 Her husband carries little peace about him.

Adurni. Fall danger what fall can, she is a goodness   50
 Above temptation, more to be adored
 Than sifted; I'm to blame, sure.

Futelli.   Levidolce,
 For her part too, laughed at Malfato's frenzy
 (Just so she termed it); but for you, my lord,
 She said she thanked your charity, which lent   55
 Her crookèd soul, before it left her body,
 Some respite wherein it might learn again
 The means of growing straight.

Adurni.   She has found mercy,
 Which I will seek, and sue for.

Futelli.   You are happy.

                                                 Exeunt.

[ACT 3 SCENE 3]

Enter AURIA *and* AURELIO.

Auria. Count of Savona, Genoa's admiral,
 Lord governor of Corsica, enrolled
 A worthy of my country, sought and sued to,
 Praised, courted, flattered! Sure, this bulk of mine
 Tails in the size; a tympany of greatness   5

---

46. *prints*] visible tracks.

47. *tongue*] audible sign, with a suggestion of hounds giving tongue when they scent a quarry.

52. *sifted*] tested, examined.

59. *sue for*] pray for.

happy] fortunate.

3. *worthy*] principal dignitary.

4. *bulk*] body.

5. *Tails*] Weber conjectured that the word meant 'entails', but *OED* (tail v.2, 9) glosses as 'tally', citing this as the sole instance. It would therefore mean something like 'my body swells proportionately to my new status'.

tympany] harmful swelling, tumour.

Puffs up too monstrously my narrow chest.
How surely dost thou malice these extremes,
Uncomfortable man! When I was needy,
Cast naked on the flats of barren pity,
Abated to an ebb so low that boys   10
A-cock-horse frisked about me without plunge,
You could chat gravely then, in formal tones,
Reason most paradoxically; now
Contempt and wilful grudge at my uprising
Becalms your learnèd noise.
Aurelio.   Such flourish, Auria,   15
Flies with so swift a gale as it will waft
Thy sudden joys into a faithless harbour.
Auria. Canst mutter, mischief? I observed your dullness
Whiles the whole ging crowed to me. Hark, my
    triumphs
Are echoed under every roof, the air   20
Is straitened with the sound, there is not room
Enough to brace them in; but not a thought
Doth pierce into the grief that cabins here.
Here through a creek, a little inlet, crawls

---

8. *Uncomfortable*] not comforting.

9. *naked*] destitute, without means.

flats] shoals, which are areas from which it is difficult to get afloat again.

11. *A-cock-horse*] Literally, riding on cock-horses, or riding astride as children did on wooden horses; metaphorically, it can also mean to triumph. Auria may mean that he saw his fortunes lagging behind those of much younger men.

plunge] being thrown off.

17. *faithless*] untrustworthy.

18–19. *Canst . . . to me*] Auria might say this aside, but I think the complete candour of his previous dealings with Aurelio means that he would not shrink from addressing him as 'mischief' to his face. He certainly does not shrink from saying harsh things later in the scene.

19. *ging*] gang, company.

21. *straitened*] constricted, impeded.

22. *brace*] turn (of a sail), leading on to the further nautical metaphor of 'cabins' in the next line.

　　A flake no bigger than a sister's thread,　　　　　25
　　Which sets the region of my heart afire.
　　I had a kingdom once, but am deposed
　　From all that royalty of blessed content
　　By a confederacy 'twixt love and frailty.
Aurelio. Glories in public view but add to misery　　30
　　Which travails in unrest at home.
Auria.　　　　　　　　　　At home?
　　That home Aurelio speaks of I have lost,
　　And which is worse, when I have rolled about,
　　Toiled like a pilgrim round this globe of earth,
　　Wearied with care, and overworn with age,　　　35
　　Lodged in the grave, I am not yet at home,
　　There rots but half of me; the other part
　　Sleeps heaven knows where. Would she and I – my wife,
　　I mean; but what, alas, talk I of wife?
　　The woman – would we had together fed　　　40
　　On any outcast parings, coarse and mouldy,
　　Not lived divided thus; I could have begged
　　For both, for't had been pity she should ever
　　Have felt so much extremity.
Aurelio.　　　　　　　　This is not
　　Patience required in wrongs of such vile nature.　　45
　　You pity her. Think rather on revenge!
Auria. Revenge! For what, uncharitable friend?
　　On whom? Let's speak a little, pray, with reason.
　　You found Spinella in Adurni's house;
　　'Tis like 'a gave her welcome, very likely.　　　50

---

25. sister's] *Q*; spider's *Gifford; restored to* sister's *by Dyce.*

---

　25. *flake*] portion of ignited matter (*OED* flake n.2), which is why Auria's heart is on fire.
　sister's thread] Dyce glossed this as 'sewster's' (sempstress's), but it could equally refer to the thread spun by the Fates controlling human lifespans in Greek mythology.
　33. *when I have rolled about*] when I have come full circle, i.e. from the cradle to the grave.
　34. *pilgrim*] one on a long journey in search of something holy.
　37. *other part*] In line with the Neoplatonic belief that each soul had a twin for which it must seek.
　41. *outcast parings*] discarded scrapings.

Her sister and another with her, so
Invited, nobly done; but he with her
Privately chambered. He deserves no wife
Of worthy quality who dares not trust
Her virtue in the proofs of any danger.   55
Aurelio. But I broke ope the doors upon 'em.
Auria.   Marry,
It was a slovenly presumption,
And punishable by a sharp rebuke.
I tell you, sir, I in my younger growth
Have by the stealth of privacy enjoyed   60
A lady's closet, where to have profaned
That shrine of chastity and innocence
With one unhallowed word would have exiled
The freedom of such favour into scorn.
Had any he alive then ventured there   65
With foul construction, I had stamped the justice
Of my unguilty truth upon his heart.
Aurelio. Adurni might have done the like, but that
The conscience of his fault in coward blood
Blushed at the quick surprisal.
Auria.   O fie, fie!   70
How ill some argue in their sour reproof
Against a party liable to law!

56–7. Marry, / It] *Weber*; Marry, it *Q*.

---

57. *slovenly*] low, lewd (*OED* a,1).
59–64.] Cf. *Othello* 4.1.3–4, with the Othello-figure ironically speaking the Iago-figure's lines.
60–1. *enjoyed/A lady's closet*] Had the privilege of being received in a lady's private room, usually reserved solely for her own use.
66. *foul construction*] interpretation which saw harm (cf. the motto of the Order of the Garter, 'honni soit qui mal y pense', shamed be he who thinks evil of it). There is an implied contrast with the good constructions which the council and the duke of Florence placed on Auria's achievements against the Turks.
stamped the justice] written the proof of the innocence. Auria would have stabbed in the heart anyone who had misconstrued his presence in the closet and would thus, according to the logic of trial by combat, have demonstrated that he, as the victor, had right on his side.

For had that lord offended with that creature,
Her presence would have doubled every strength
Of man in him, and justified the forfeit   75
Of noble shame; else 'twas enough in both
With a smile only to correct your rudeness.
Aurelio. 'Tis well you make such use of neighbours' courtesy.
 Some kind of beasts are tame, and hug their injuries;
 Such way leads to a fame too.
Auria.   Not uncivilly,   80
 Though violently, friend.
Aurelio.   Wherefore then, think ye,
 Can she absent herself, if she be blameless?
 You grant, of course, your triumphs are proclaimed,
 And I in person told her your return.
 Where lies she hid the while?
Auria.   That rests for answer   85
 In you. Now I come t'ee. We have exchanged
 Bosoms, Aurelio, from our years of childhood;
 Let me acknowledge with what pride I own
 A man so faithful, honest, fast my friend –
 He whom, if I speak fully, never failed,   90
 By teaching trust to me, to learn of mine.
 I wished myself thine equal; if I aimed
 A wrong, 'twas in an envy of thy goodness.
 So dearly, witness with me my integrity,
 I laid thee up to heart, that from my love   95
 My wife was but distinguished in her sex.

73–7.] If Adurni really had misbehaved himself with Spinella, the fact
that she was there would have hugely emboldened him, and blinded him to
any consideration of shame; as it was, it was perfectly reasonable for both of
them not to dignify your rudeness with anything more than a contemptuous
smile.

79. *tame*] meek, subservient.

hug their injuries] keep their wrongs to themselves.

80. *Such . . . too*] Behaviour like that also gets you a reputation (but by
implication not a good one).

92–3 *aimed/A wrong*] committed bad behaviour. It is tempting to see here
a reference to the Aristotelian idea that the 'flaw' of a tragic hero is a *hamartia*, a taking of false aim.

Give back that holy signature of friendship
Cancelled, defaced, plucked off, or I shall urge
Accounts scored on the tally of my vengeance,
Without all former compliments.
Aurelio.   D'ee imagine   100
I fawn upon your fortunes, or intrude
Upon the hope of bettering my estate,
That you cashier me at a minute's warning?
No, Auria, I dare vie with your respects:
Put both into the balance, and the poise   105
Shall make a settled stand. Perhaps the proffer
So frankly vowed at your departure first
Of settling me a partner in your purchase
Leads you into opinion of some ends
Of mercenary falsehood; yet such wrong   110
Least suits a noble soul.
Auria.   By all my sorrows,
The mention is too coarse.
Aurelio.   Since then th'occasion
Presents our discontinuance, use your liberty.
For my part I am resolute to die
The same my life professed me.
Auria.   Pish, your faith   115
Was never in suspicion. But consider,

---

97. *signature*] distinguishing mark. Auria's metaphor may evoke the idea
of things which are greatly valued being written on the heart.

97–100. *Give . . . compliments*] Restore the friendship which you have vio-
lated or I shall hold you accountable and take my revenge accordingly
without any more fine words.

98–9. *urge / Accounts*] demand a settling-up.

99. *scored*] marked, notched (usually in a tavern).

tally] stick of wood on which the number of notches made represented
the amount of money owed. Again, the language of money and trade accrues
to conversations about Spinella. In *The Broken Heart*, Ithocles muses that
'So provident is folly in sad issue/That after-wit, like bankrupts' debts, stand
tallied/Without all possibilities of payment' (4.1.11–13).

103. *cashier*] dismiss. The word recalls *Othello*, where Cassio is cashiered
as Othello's lieutenant.

105–6. *Put . . . stand*] Put both into the scales, and their equal weight will
cause the scales to hang level.

108.] Aurelio is referring to Auria's offer to make him his heir.

113. *use your liberty*] do what you like.

Neither the lord nor lady, nor the bawd
Which shuffled them together, opportunity,
Have fastened stain on my unquestioned name;
My friend's rash indiscretion was the bellows   120
Which blew the coal, now kindled to a flame
Will light his slander to all wandering eyes.
Some men in giddy zeal o'erdo that office
They catch at, of whose number is Aurelio.
For I am certain, certain it had been   125
Impossible, had you stood wisely silent,
But my Spinella, trembling on her knee,
Would have accused her breach of truth, have begged
A speedy execution on her trespass.
Then with a justice lawful as the magistrates'   130
Might I have drawn my sword against Adurni,
Which now is sheathed and rusted in the scabbard.
Good thanks to your cheap providence! Once more
I make demand – my wife – you – sir –
                              [*Draws his sword.*]
Aurelio.   Roar louder,
The noise affrights not me; threaten your enemies,   135
And prove a valiant tongue-man – now must follow,
By way of method, the exact condition
Of rage which runs to mutiny in friendship.
Auria, come on; this weapon looks not pale
                              [*Draws his sword.*]
At sight of that. Again hear and believe it: 140
What I have done was well done and well meant;
Twenty times over, were it new to do,
I'd do't and do't, and boast the pains religious;
Yet since you shake me off, I slightly value
Other severity.

121–2.] Aurelio's indiscreet publicising of the matter first sparked scandal, which is now burning merrily and drawing everyone's attention.

127. *But*] but that – i.e. if Aurelio had kept quiet, it would have been impossible for Spinella not to have knelt and confessed.

136. *tongue-man*] talker.

143 *boast the pains religious*] say the endeavour was a just one.

Auria.   Honour and duty   145
   Stand my compurgators, never did passion
   Purpose ungentle usage of my sword
   Against Aurelio. Let me rather want
                   [Both sheathe their swords.]
   My hands, nay, friend, a heart, than ever suffer
   Such dotage enter here; if I must lose   150
   Spinella, let me not proceed to misery
   By losing my Aurelio. We through madness
   Frame strange conceits in our discoursing brains
   And prate of things as we pretend they were;
   Join help to mine, good man, and let us listen   155
   After this straying soul, and till we find her,
   Bear our discomfort quietly.
Aurelio.   So doubtless
   She may be soon discovered.
Auria.   That's spoke cheerfully.
   Why there's a friend now! Auria and Aurelio
   At odds? Oh't cannot be, must not, and sha'not –   160

              Enter CASTANNA.

   But look, Castanna's here! Welcome, fair figure
   Of a choice jewel, locked up in a cabinet,
   More precious than the public view should sully.
Castanna. Sir, how you are informed, or on what terms
   Of prejudice against my course or custom   165
   Opinion sways your confidence, I know not;
   Much anger, if my fears persuade not falsely,
   Sits on this gentleman's stern brow; yet, sir,
   If an unhappy maid's word may find credit,
   As I wish harm to nobody on earth,   170
   So would all good folks may wish none to me.

---

146. *compurgators*] people who testify to the innocence of another. Auria swears by his honour and duty that he intended no harm to Aurelio.

150. *dotage*] folly.

155–6. *let ... soul*] let us see if we can hear anything of this wandering creature.

161–3. *fair ... sully*] image of a precious gem kept in a private place because it is too good to be generally seen; cf. the Marquis's figuring of his nieces as privately kept jewels in *The Fancies Chaste and Noble* 5.3.37–9.

Auria. None does, sweet sister.
Castanna.   If they do, dear heaven
      Forgive them is my prayer; but perhaps
      You might conceive – and yet methinks you should not –
      How I am faulty in my sister's absence;   175
      Indeed 'tis nothing so, nor was I knowing
      Of any private speech my lord intended,
      Save civil entertainment. Pray what hurt
      Can fall out in discourse, if it be modest?
      Sure noble men will show that they are such   180
      With those of their own rank, and that was all
      My sister can be charged with.
Auria.   Is't not, friend,
      An excellent maid?
Aurelio.   Deserves the best of fortunes;
      I ever spoke her virtuous.
Castanna.   With your leave,
      You used most cruel language to my sister,   185
      Enough to fright her wits; not very kind
      To me myself. She sighed when you were gone,
      Desired no creature else should follow her;
      And in good truth, I was so full of weeping,
      I marked not well which way she went.
Auria.   Stayed she not   190
      Within the house then?
Castanna.   'Las, not she – Aurelio
      Was passing rough.
Auria.   Strange! Nowhere to be found out?
Castanna. Not yet; but, on my life, ere many hours
      I shall hear from her.
Auria.   Shalt thou? Worthy maid,
      Th'ast brought to my sick heart a cordial. – Friend,   195
      Good news. – Most sweet Castanna!
Aurelio.   May it prove so.
                              Exeunt.

182–3. friend, / An] *Weber;* friend, an *Q.*

---

   173. *prayer*] Disyllabic. This is perhaps another marker of the Devon-born
Ford's accent, as with his tendency to make 'girl' and 'pearl' disyllabic.
   192. *passing rough*] exceedingly harsh.
   195. *cordial*] medicine to invigorate the heart.

[ACT 3 SCENE 4]

Enter BENAZZI *as before.*

Benazzi. The paper in the purse for my directions appointed
this the place, the time now; here dance I attendance. She
is come already.

Enter LEVIDOLCE.

Levidolce. Parado – so I overheard you named.
Benazzi. A mushroom sprung up in a minute by the sunshine   5
of your benevolent grace. Liberality and hospitable compassion, most magnificent beauty, have long since lain
bedrid in the ashes of the old world till now. Your illustri-
ous charity hath raked up the dead embers by giving life
to a worm inevitably devoted yours as you shall please to   10
new-shape me.
Levidolce. A grateful man, it seems. Where gratitude
Has harbour, other furniture becoming
Accomplished qualities must needs inhabit.
What country claims your birth?   15
Benazzi. None: I was born at sea, as my mother was in
passage from Cape Lugodori to Cape Cagliari toward
Afric in Sardinia, was bred up in Aquilastro, and at
years put myself in service under the Spanish viceroy, till
I was taken prisoner by the Turks. I have tasted in my   20
days handsome store of good and bad, and am thankful
for both.
Levidolce. You seem the issue then of honest parents.
Benazzi. Reputed no less; many children oftentimes inherit
their lands who peradventure never begot them. My   25

17. Lugodori] *This ed.*; Ludugory *Q.*

5. *mushroom*] Proverbial for rapid growth, and hence a common term for
an upstart.
8. *bedrid*] confined to bed.
17. *Cape Lugodori*] Q's 'Ludugory' is clearly Ford's approximation of
Lugodori, which with Cagliari was one of the two capes which contemporary
maps showed in Sardinia.
17–18. *toward Afric*] i.e. sailing southwards towards Africa.
18. *Aquilastro*] The name occurs on Mercator's 1554 map of Sardinia.
24–5. *inherit ... them*] inherit the lands of men who quite possibly did not
actually father them.

mother's husband was a very old man at my birth, but
no man is too old to father his wife's child. Your servant
I am sure I will ever prove myself entirely.

Levidolce. Dare you be secret?

Benazzi.   Yes.

Levidolce.   And sudden?

Benazzi.   Yes.

Levidolce. But withal sure of hand and spirit?

Benazzi.   Yes, yes, yes.   30

Levidolce. I use not many words; the time prevents 'em.
    A man of quality has robbed mine honour.

Benazzi. Name him.

Levidolce.   Adurni.

Benazzi.   'A shall bleed.

Levidolce.   Malfato
    Contemned my proffered love.

Benazzi.   Yoke 'em in death.
    What's my reward?

Levidolce.   Propose it, and enjoy it.   35

Benazzi. You for my wife.

Levidolce.   Ha!

Benazzi.   Nothing else; deny me
    And I'll betray your counsels, to your ruin;
    Else do the feat courageously. Consider.

29–36.] *Gifford; probably prose in Q, though Q does not mark half-lines sepa-*
rately.   30. yes, yes, yes] *Q*; yes, yes *Gifford.*

---

27. *no man … child*] It was the presumption in law that any child born to
a married woman was begotten by her husband, a test case for this being
the long-running legal wrangle about the succession to the earldom of
Banbury. On 10 April 1627, when her husband was eighty-two years old, the
countess of Banbury, who was known to be the mistress of Edward, fourth
Baron Vaux, bore a son, followed by a second son in 1631. When the earl
died in 1632 (the countess married Vaux five weeks later), a dispute, which
rumbled on for the next two centuries, arose about the two boys' paternity
and hence their eligibility to succeed. Ford would have been interested in
this both because of his residence at the Middle Temple and also because
the earl was the uncle of Rober Devereux, second earl of Essex, a figure who
fascinated Ford.

29–30.] Once again Benazzi matches his interlocutor by speaking verse.

Levidolce. I do; dispatch the task I have enjoined,
    Then claim my promise.
Benazzi.   No such matter, pretty one;   40
    We'll marry first, or farewell.
Levidolce.   Stay. Examine
    From my confession what a plague thou drawst
    Into thy bosom: though I blush to say it,
    Know I have without sense of shame or honour
    Forsook a lawful marriage bed to dally   45
    Between Adurni's arms.
Benazzi.   This lord's.
Levidolce.   The same;
    More, not content with him, I courted
    A newer pleasure, but was there refused
    By him I named so late.
Benazzi.   Malfato.
Levidolce.   Right.
    Am henceforth resolutely bent to print   50
    My follies on their hearts, then change my life
    For some rare penance. Canst thou love me now?
Benazzi. Better; I do believe 'tis possible you may mend.
    All this breaks off no bargain.
Levidolce. Accept my hand; with this a faith as constant   55
    As vows can urge. Nor shall my haste prevent
    This contract, which death only must divorce.
Benazzi. Settle the time.
Levidolce.   Meet here tomorrow night;
    We will determine further, as behoves us.

46–7. same; / More] *Weber*; same; more *Q.*   49–50. Right. / Am] *Weber*; Right, am *Q.*   53.] *Q*; Better: / I *Gifford; prose Weber, Nogami.*   53–4.] *Q*; prose *Nogami.*

50–2. *Am ... penance*] From now on I am determined (first) to kill Malfato and Adurni, whose deaths will bear witness to my mistakes, then change my present way of existence for a notable penance. Levidolce would thus become the same sort of reformed sinner as Giuliano Adorno, husband of St Catherine of Genoa, who was converted from a life of sin to one of holiness.

Benazzi. How is my new love called?

Levidolce.   Levidolce.   60
    Be confident, I bring a worthy portion;
    But you'll fly off.

Benazzi.   Not I, by all that's noble;
    A kiss – farewell – dear fate.   *Exit.*

Levidolce.   Love is sharp-sighted
    And can pierce through the cunning of disguises.
    False pleasures, I cashier ye; fair truth, welcome.   *Exit.*   65

60–1. Levidolce. / Be] *Weber (subst.); Levidolche,* be *Q.*

62. *you'll fly off*] you won't keep your part of the bargain.

63–5. *Love ... welcome*] Levidolce makes it clear here that she has recognised Benazzi as her husband and really does mean to renounce her former ways.

Act 4

Enter MALFATO *and* SPINELLA.

Malfato. Here you are safe, sad cousin; if you please
    May over-say the circumstance of what
    You late discoursed. Mine ears are gladly open,
    For I myself am in such hearty league
    With solitary thoughts that pensive language   5
    Charms my attention.
Spinella.   But my husband's honours,
    By how much more in him they sparkle clearly,
    By so much more they tempt belief to credit
    The wrack and ruin of my injured name.
Malfato. Why, cousin, should the earth cleave to the roots,   10
    The seas and heavens be mingled in disorder,
    Your purity with unaffrighted eyes
    Might wait the uproar; 'tis the guilty trembles
    At horrors, not the innocent. You are cruel
    In censuring a liberty allowed.   15
    Speak freely, gentle cousin: was Adurni
    Importunately wanton?
Spinella.   In excess
    Of entertainment, else not.
Malfato.   Not the boldness
    Of an uncivil courtship?
Spinella.   What that meant
    I never understood. I have at once   20
    Set bars between my best of earthly joys,
    And best of men, so excellent a man

---

2. *over-say*] repeat.
6–9.] This difficult passage would appear to mean that Auria's new-found
eminence will act as a spur to encourage backbiters to latch on to some cause
to bring him down.

    As lives, without comparison; his love
    To me was matchless.
Malfato.   Yet put case, sweet cousin,
    That I could name a creature whose affection   25
    Followed your Auria in the height; affection
    To you, even to Spinella, true and settled
    As ever Auria's was, can, is, or will be.
    You may not chide the story.
Spinella.   Fortune's minions
    Are flattered, not the miserable.
Malfato.   Listen   30
    To a strange tale, which thus the author sighed:
    A kinsman of Spinella – so it runs –
    Her father's sister's son, some time before
    Auria the fortunate possessed her beauties,
    Became enamoured of such rare perfections   35
    As she was stored with; fed his idle hopes
    With possibilities of lawful conquest;
    Proposed each difficulty in pursuit
    Of what his vain supposal styled his own;
    Found in the argument one only flaw   40
    Of conscience, by the nearness of their bloods –
    Unhappy scruple, easily dispensed with,
    Had any friend's advice resolved the doubt.
    Still on 'a loved and loved, and wished and wished,
    Eftsoon began to speak, yet soon broke off,   45
    And still the fondling durst not, cause 'a durst not.
Spinella. 'Twas wonderful.
Malfato.   Exceeding wonderful,
    Beyond all wonder; yet 'tis known for truth.
    After her marriage, when remained not aught
    Of expectation to such fruitless dotage,   50
    His reason then – now – then could not reduce
    The violence of passion, though 'a vowed
    Never to unlock that secret, scarce to her

---

53. Never] *Q*; Ne'er *Gifford*.

33.] Cf. the earlier stress on uncles (2.2.59–60).
45. *Eftsoon*] periodically.
46. *fondling*] fool.
47. *wonderful*] extraordinary.

          Herself, Spinella, and withal resolved
          Not to come near her presence, but to avoid   55
          All opportunities however proffered.
Spinella. An understanding dulled by th'infelicity
          Of constant sorrow is not apprehensive
          In pregnant novelty; my ears receive
          The words you utter, cousin, but my thoughts   60
          Are fastened on another subject.
Malfato.   Can
          You embrace, so like a darling, your own woes,
          And play the tyrant with a partner in them?
          Then I am thankful for advantage: urged
          By fatal and enjoined necessity   65
          To stand up in defence of injured virtue,
          Will against any – I except no quality –
          Maintain all supposition misapplied,
          Unhonest, false and villainous.
Spinella.   Dear cousin,
          As you're a gentleman –
Malfato.   I'll bless that hand   70
          Whose honourable pity seals the passport
          For my incessant turmoils to their rest.
          If I prevail – which heaven forbid – these ages
          Which shall inherit ours may tell posterity
          Spinella had Malfato for a kinsman,   75
          By noble love made jealous of her fame.
Spinella. No more; I dare not hear it.
Malfato.   All is said:

61–2. Can / You embrace] _Weber;_ Can you embrace _Q;_ Can you / Embrace
Gifford. 64. advantage] _Q;_ [th']adavantage _Gifford._ 69–70. cousin, /
As] _Weber;_ cousin, as _Q._ 70. you're] _Weber;_ y'are _Q._

58. _apprehensive_] able to take in.
59. _pregnant novelty_] important news.
61–3. _Can ... them?_] Malfato reproaches Spinella with making a beloved
object of her own sorrow but ignoring the fact that he too is suffering.
64. _advantage_] opportunity.
67. _quality_] class of people.
69. _Unhonest_] unseemly, lewd.
70–2. _I'll ... rest_] I will be grateful to the hand which sends my sorrows
to the grave. Malfato hopes to die in the duel he thinks of fighting because
it will bring his sufferings to an end.

Henceforth shall never syllable proceed
From my unpleasant voice of amorous folly

Enter CASTANNA.

Castanna. Your summons warned me hither; I am come.   80
Sister, my sister, 'twas an unkind part
Not to take me along w'ee.
Malfato.   Chide her for it;
Castanna, this house is as freely yours
As ever was your father's.
Castanna.   We conceive so,
Though your late strangeness hath bred marvel in us.   85
But wherefore, sister, keeps your silence distance?
Am I not welcome t'ee?
Spinella.   Lives Auria safe?
Oh, prithee do not hear me call him husband
Before thou canst resolve what kind of wife
His fury terms the runaway. Speak quickly!   90
Yet do not – stay. Castanna, I am lost;
His friend hath set before him a bad woman,
And he, good man, believes it.
Castanna.   Now in truth –
Spinella. Hold, my heart trembles; I perceive thy tongue
Is great with ills and hastes to be delivered.   95
I should not use Castanna so. First tell me,
Shortly and truly tell me how he does.
Castanna. In perfect health.
Spinella.   For that my thanks to heaven.

79.1.] *This ed.; in Q this appears in the margin next to ll. 78–9.*   82. w'ee] *Q*;
wi'you *Weber*; w'ye *Gifford*; wi'ee *Nogami.*

---

79. *unpleasant*] displeasing, unwelcome. Gifford put a full stop at the end
of this speech of Malfato's, and, in one of his rare comments, observes that
'Malfato has hitherto appeared to little advantage; but the author makes him
full amends in this beautiful scene'. Q, however, has a long dash, suggesting
that Malfato is interrupted by the arrival of Castanna, and that had he not
been, he might in fact have said more despite his protestations that he was
not about to do so.
82. *w'ee*] with you.
95. *great with*] pregnant with.

Malfato. The world hath not another wife like this.
    Cousin, you will not hear your sister speak,   100
    So much your passion rules.
Spinella.   Even what she pleases;
    Go on, Castanna.
Castanna.   Your most noble husband
    Is deaf to all reports, and only grieves
    At his soul's love Spinella's causeless absence.
Malfato. Why look ye, cousin, now!
Spinella.   Indeed?
Castanna.   Will value   105
    No counsel, takes no pleasure in his greatness,
    Neither admits of likelihood at all
    That you are living; if you were he's certain
    It were impossible you could conceal
    Your welcomes to him, being all one with him.   110
    But as for jealousy of your dishonour,
    He both laughs at and scorns it.
Spinella.   Does 'a?
Malfato.   Therein
    He shows himself desertful of his happiness.
Castanna. Methinks the news should cause some motion,
      sister.
    You are not well.
Malfato.   Not well?
Spinella.   I am unworthy.   115
Malfato. Of whom? What? Why?
Spinella.   Go, cousin; come, Castanna.
                         Exeunt.

[ACT 4 SCENE 2]

Enter TRELCATIO, PIERO *and* FUTELLI.

Trelcatio. The state in council is already set;
    My coming will be late. Now therefore, gentlemen,

---

113. *desertful*] deserving.
114. *motion*] reaction.

This house is free. As your intents are sober,
Your pains shall be accepted.
Futelli.   Mirth sometimes
Falls into earnest, signor.
Piero.   We for our parts   5
Aim at the best.
Trelcatio.   You wrong yourselves and me else;
Good success t'ee.   *Exit.*
Piero. Futelli, 'tis our wisest course to follow
Our pastime with discretion, by which means
We may ingratiate, as our business hits,   10
Our undertakings to great Auria's favour.
Futelli. I grow quite weary of this lazy custom,
Attending on the fruitless hopes of service
For meat and rags. A wit? A shrewd preferment!
Study some scurril jests, grow old and beg!   15
No, let 'em be admired that love foul linen.
I'll run a new course.
Piero.   Get the coin we spend,
And knock 'em o'er the pate who jeers our earnings –
Futelli. Husht man, one suitor comes.
                                                    Music.
Piero.   The t'other follows.

                    Enter AMORETTA.

Futelli. Be not so loud – here comes Madonna Sweet-lips.   20
Mithtreth inthooth, forthooth, will lithp it to uth.

4–7.] *Weber; prose in Q.*   18. jeers] *Q;* jeer *Weber.*

3. *free*] available to be freely used.
4. *pains*] efforts.
7.] a half line.
11.] Because Amoretta is Auria's cousin (a plan which eventually proves
successful).
14. *rags*] shabby clothes, perhaps cast-offs.
15. *scurril*] A short form of scurrilous.
16. *admired*] wondered at.
foul linen] dirty undergarments.
17. *Get*] earn.
18. *pate*] head.
jeers] Weber and Gifford silently emended to *jeer*, to agree with the plural
'em, but the construction seems flexible enough to admit of a certain loose-
ness in this respect.

Amoretta. Dentlemen, then ye; ith thith muthic yourth,
      Or can ye tell what great man'th fiddleth made it?
      'Tith vedee petty noithe, but who thould thend it?
Piero. Does not yourself know, lady?
Amoretta.   I do not uthe   25
      To thpend lip labour upon quethtionth
      That I mythelf can anthwer.
Futelli.   No, sweet madam,
      Your lips are destined to a better use,
      Or else the proverb fails of lisping maids.
Amoretta. Kithing you mean; pway, come behind with your
         mockth then,   30
      My lipth will therve the one to kith the other –
      How now, what'th neckt?

SONG.

      What ho, we come to be merry!
      Open the doors! A jovial crew,
      Lusty boys and free, and very,   35
      Very, very lusty boys are we!
      We can drink till all look blue,

22–4.] *Gifford; prose in Q.*   30. *pway*] *This ed.*; pey *Q*; pay *Weber.*

22. *then ye*] Amoretta's lisped version of 'den ye', a contracted and inverted form of 'God give you good even[ing]'.

30.] Girls who lisped were proverbially said to be good kisses.

come behind] come on after. Amoretta goodhumouredly invites them to carry on making sport of her.

31.] Amoretta seems to be referring here to her lisp, and the way her lips rub against each other, as well as making the point that she will be 'kissing' herself rather than Futelli or Piero.

32.] a half line.

SONG] Again William Lawes's score survives, this time in BM. ADD. MS. 31432, 4.18 (see Nogami, Appendix D, and John P. Cutts, 'British Museum Additional MS. 31432: William Lawes' writing for the theatre and the court', *The Library* (5th series) 7 (1952). 225–35, p. 230).

34. *a jovial crew*] This is the title of a play by Richard Brome, who seems to be remembered elsewhere in the play in the use of the name 'Snortenfert', also found in Brome. However, the phrase 'jovial crew' is not unique to Brome; Matthew Steggle points to its occurrence in William Blunden's 1636 ballad 'Hang Pinching, or, The Good fellows Observation, Mongst a Joviall Crew, Of them that hate Flinching, but is always true blew', and also suggests that many later 'jovial crew' ballads 'are interested in the practice of paying for your friends as well as yourself' (Steggle 171–2).

    Dance, sing, and roar,
    Never give o'er
    As long as we have e'er an eye to see.　　　　40
    Pithee, pithee, leth's come in.
    One thall all oua favours win.
    Dently, dently, we thall pass.
    None kitheth like the lithping lass.

Piero. What, call ye this a song?　　　　45
Amoretta. Yeth, a delithious thong, and wondrouth pretty.
Futelli. [*Aside*] A very country catch! [*To Amoretta*] Doubtless
    some prince
  Belike hath sent it to congratulate
  Your night's repose.
Amoretta.　　　　　　　　Think ye tho, thignor?
  It muth be then thome unknown obthcure printh　　　　50
  That thunth the light.
Piero.　　　　　　　　　　Perhaps the prince of darkness.
Amoretta. Of darkneth? What ith he?
Futelli.　　　　　　　　　　A courtier matchless:
  'A woos and wins more beauties to his love
  Than all the kings on earth.
Amoretta.　　　　　　　　Whea thtandth hith court, pway –

            Enter FULGOSO.

Futelli. This gentleman approaching, I presume,　　　　55
  Has more relation to his court than I,
  And comes in time t'inform ye.
Amoretta.　　　　　　　　　　Think ye tho?
  I'm thure you know him.
Piero.　　　　　　　　　Lady, you'll perceive it.

---

40. e'er] *Gifford*; ne'er *Q*.　46. thong] *Nogami*; thing *Q*.　54. pway] *This ed.*; pey *Q*; pay *Gifford*.　57–8. tho? / I'm] *Weber*; tho? ime *Q*.

41–4.] The singers' apparent mockery of Amoretta turns to flattery as they imply a link between lisping and excellence in kissing.
45.] a half line.
47. *country catch*] rustic song, probably with a pun on 'cunt'.
48. *congratulate*] express gratification at.
51. *thunth*] Amoretta's lisping version of 'shuns'.
the prince of darkness] Piero alludes to the idea that the devil is a gentleman; there is also a glance at the idea of persuading Amoretta to do 'the deed of darkness'.

Fulgoso. She seems in my first entrance to admire me;
 Protest, she eyes me round! Fulg, she's thine own. 60
Piero. Noble Fulgoso!
Fulgoso.   Did you hear the music?
 'Twas I that brought it. Was't not tickling, ah ha?
Amoretta. Pway what pinth thent it?
Fulgoso.   Prince? No prince but we.
 We set the ditty and composed the song.
 There's not a note or foot in't but our own, 65
 And the pure-trodden mortar of this brain.
 We can do things and things.
Amoretta.   Dood, thing't youathelf then.
Fulgoso. Nay, nay, I could never sing
 More than a gib-cat, or a very howlet,
 But you shall hear me whistle it.
Amoretta.   Thith thing'th thome jethter; 70
 Thure he belongth unto the printh of darkneth.
Piero. Yes, and I'll tell you what his office is:
 His prince delights himself exceedingly
 In birds of diverse kinds; this gentleman
 Is keeper and instructor of his blackbirds. 75
 He took his skill first from his father's carter.

---

60. she's] *Weber*; shees is *Q.* 63. Pway] *This ed.*; Pay *Q.* pinth] *Q*; printh *Gifford.* 65. not] *Weber*; nos *Q.* 74. diverse] *This ed.*; divers *Q.* 75–6.] *Weber*; prose in *Q.*

 60. *Protest*] I protest.
 62. *tickling*] stirring.
 63. *pinth*] Amoretta now seems to be dropping her r sounds as well as lisping, though it may just be that the compositor has made a mistake because of the difficulty of the material (see Introduction, **p. 30**).
 66. *mortar*] cohesive material.
 68.] a half line.
 69. *gib-cat*] Gib is a common term for a cat, especially a castrated one.
 howlet] owl; also used for someone who is gullible. The term is often applied specifically to female owls, reinforcing the sense of effeminisation attached to Fulgoso here.
 75. *instructor of his blackbirds*] blackbirds are easily trained and can subsequently make valued pets.
 76. *carter*] driver of a cart. The implication is that Fulgoso is employed solely on menial tasks.

Amoretta. 'Tith wonderful to thee by what thtrange means
    Thome men are raised to platheth.
Fulgoso.   I do hear you,
    And thank ye heartily for your good wills
    In setting forth my parts; but what I live on   80
    Is simple trade of money from my lands.
    Hang sharks, I am no shifter.
Amoretta.   Ith't pothible –

Enter GUZMAN.

    Bleth uth, who'th thith?
Futelli.   Oh, it is the man of might.
Guzman. May my address to beauty lay no scandal
    Upon my martial honour, since even Mars,   85
    Whom as in war, in love I imitate,
    Could not resist the shafts of Cupid; therefore,
    As with the god of war, I deign to stoop.
    Lady, vouchsafe, love's-goddess-like, to yield
    Your fairer hand unto these lips, the portals   90
    Of valiant breath that hath o'erturned an army.
Amoretta. Faya weather keep me, what a thtorm ith thith?
Futelli. O don, keep off at further distance – yet
    A little farther. Do you not observe
    How your strong breath hath terrified the lady?   95
Guzman. I'll stop the breath of war and breathe as gently
    As a perfumèd pair of sucking bellows
    In some sweet lady's chamber, for I can
    Speak lion-like, or sheep-like, when I please.
Futelli. Stand by then without noise a while, brave don,   100
    And let her only view your parts; they'll take her.
Guzman. I'll publish them in silence.
Piero.   Stand you there,

---

82. Ith't] *Nogami*; Ith *Q*.

---

82. *sharks*] spongers, parasites who gain their living by swindling or cheating (Cf. *The Alchemist* 1.1.160, 'prove today, who shall shark best').
    shifter] trickster, cozener.
    90–1. *portals ... army*] Guzman apparently has bad breath, as Futelli
observes at l. 95.
    97.] Presumably a device for pumping perfume into a room is envisaged.
    102. *publish*] put on show.

Fulgoso the magnificent.

Fulgoso.   Here?

Piero.   Just there.

Let her survey you both; you'll be her choice,

Ne'er doubt it, man.

Fulgoso.   I cannot doubt it, man.   105

Piero. But speak not till I bid you.

Fulgoso.   I may whistle?

Piero. A little to yourself, to spend the time.

Amoretta. [*Aside*] Both foolth, you thay?

Futelli.   [*Aside*] But hear them for your sport.

Piero. Don shall begin – begin, don; she has surveyed

Your outwards and your inwards through the rents   110

And wounds of your apparel.

Guzman.   She is politic.

My outside, lady, shrouds a prince obscured.

Amoretta. I thank ye for your muthic, printh.

Guzman.   My words

Are music to her.

Amoretta.   The muthic and the thong

You thent me by thith whithling thing, your man.   115

Guzman. [*Aside*] She took him for my man. Love, thou

wert just!

Fulgoso. I wo'not hold! His man? 'Tis time to speak

Before my time. Oh, scurvy! I his man?

That has no means for meat or rags, and seam-rents?

Guzman. Have I with this one rapier –

Piero.   He has no other.   120

Guzman. Passed through a field of pikes, whose heads

I   lopped

As easily as the bloody-minded youth

---

105. *Fulgoso*] *Weber*; FUT. Q.

110. *rents*] tears.

117–18.] Fulgoso is outraged by the suggestion that he might be the
servant of the penniless Guzman.

119. *seam-rents*] tears in his seams.

122. *the bloody-minded youth*] Sextus Tarquin, who consulted his father on
the best means of subduing the city of Gabii. The elder Tarquin received the
message in his garden, and immediately decapitated the tallest plants there,
which his son interpreted as meaning that he should kill the chief men of
the city. The incident is recounted by Thomas Heywood in his play *The Rape
of Lucrece*, scene 7, ll. 98–110.

Lopped off the poppy heads –
Fulgoso.   The puppet heads.
Guzman. Have I – have I – have I?
Fulgoso.   Thou liest, thou hast not,
    And I'll maintain't.
Guzman.   Have I – but let that pass;
    For though my famous acts were damned to silence,   125
    Yet my descent shall crown me thy superior.
Amoretta. That I would lithen to.
Guzman.   List and wonder:
    My great great grandsire was an ancient duke,
    Styled Desvergonzado.
Futelli.   That's in Spanish
    An incorrigible rogue without a fellow,   130
    An unmatched rogue. He thinks we understand not.
Guzman. So was my grandfather, hight Argozile.
Fulgoso. An arrant, arrant thief-leader; pray mock it.
Guzman. My grandsire by the mother's side a *conde*,
    Conde Scrivano.   135
Futelli.   A crop-eared scrivener.

---

125. maintain't] *Weber*; mayn't *Q.*   130. Desvergonzado] *This ed.*; Dis? vir
di Gonzado *Q*; Dis vir di Gonzado *Weber*; Desver di Gonzado *Gifford; Dis
vir di Gonzado Nogami.*   134. mock] *Q; Gifford silently changed this to mark;
Dyce noted the change but let it stand.*

---

123. *puppet heads*] In *Don Quixote*, the hero decapitates some of the
puppets he sees in a show; Fulgoso may think this an appropriate episode
with which to taunt the Spanish Guzman.

124. *Thou liest*] Fulgoso gives Guzman the lie direct.

125. *but let that pass*] This phrase is mocked by Jonson in *Every Man Out
of His Humour* (3.1.93, 3.1.372–3) and by Shakespeare in *Love's Labour's Lost*
(5.1.99 and 103).

130. *Desvergonzado*] Spanish for shameless.

133. *hight*] called.

Argozile] Weber's suggestion that this might be a corruption of *alguazil*, a
beadle, may well be correct, since Mateo Alemán's *The Rogue*, which seems
to be a source of several of the names in the play, speaks of 'an *Alguazil*, who
is a comon Catch-pole, or apprehender of mens persons' (Alemán, III, p.
233), and the eponymous hero, Guzman de Alfarache, frequently has trouble
with these officers.

135. *conde*] Spanish count.

136. *crop-eared*] having had part of his ears removed as a judicial
punishment.

scrivener] professional scribe, a job held in low repute.

Guzman. Whose son, my mother's father, was a marquis,
　Hijo de puta.
Piero.　　　　That's the son of a whore.
Guzman. And my renownèd sire Don Picaro –
Futelli. In proper sense a rascal – oh, brave don!　　　140
Guzman. Hijo de una pravada.
Piero.　　　　　　　'A goes on,
　Son of a branded bitch – high-spirited don!
Guzman. Had honours both by sea and land, to wit –
Futelli. The galleys and Bridewell.
Fulgoso.　　　　　　I'll not endure it,
　To hear a canting mongrel – hear me, lady!　　　145
Guzman. 'Tis no fair play.
Fulgoso.　　　　　I care not: fair or foul,
　I from a king derive my pedigree,
　King Oberon by name, from whom my father,
　The mighty and courageous Mountibanco,
　Was lineally descended, and my mother,　　　150
　In right of whose blood I must ever honour
　The lower Germany, was a Harlequin.

---

138. *puta*] *This ed.*; puto *Q.*　139.] *Weber; Q omits the speech prefix for*
Guzman.　Picaro] *Weber*; Piccaco *Q.*　141. *pravada*] *Weber*; pravado *Q.*

---

139. Guzman] Q omits the speech prefix here so that this line appears as
part of Piero's speech, but there can be no doubt that it belongs to Guzman,
since it is part of his catalogue of his ancestors.

Picaro] rogue. The phrase occurs several times in Mateo Alemán's *The*
Rogue, a possible source of the names Guzman and Castanna, which *OED*
cites as the first text to use the word in English. *La vida de Lazarillo de Tormes*
(1554) was the first of many narratives of the lives of rogues, a genre which
ultimately becomes known as the picaresque.

144. *galleys*] ships rowed by conscripts and prisoners.

Bridewell] a London prison, located beside the Fleet Ditch at the point
where it discharged into the Thames. Its location is marked by the present
Bridewell Place, near Blackfriars Bridge.

145. *canting*] speaking the jargon of thieves.

146. *fair or foul*] for better or worse.

148. *Oberon*] King of the fairies. This may be another oblique glance at
The Alchemist, where Dol Common impersonates the queen of the fairies.

149. *Mountibanco*] itinerant showman.

152. *lower Germany*] strictly speaking, the northern, less mountainous
parts of Germany where Low German is spoken, but sometimes (and probably here) used for the Low Countries (Netherlands).

Harlequin] stock character from the *commedia dell'arte*.

Futelli. He blow up
  The Spaniard presently by his mother-side.
Fulgoso. Her father was Grave Hans van Herne, the son   155
  Of Hogen Mogen, dat de droats did sneighen
  Of veirteen hundred Spaniards in one neict.
Guzman. Oh, diabolo!
Fulgoso. Ten thousand devils nor diabolos
  Shall fright me from my pedigree: my uncle,   160
  Yacob van Flagon-Draught, with Abraham Snortenfert
  And youngster Brogen-foh, with fourscore harquebus,
  Managed by well-lined butter-boxes, took
  A thousand Spanish jobbernowls by surprise,
  And beat a sconce about their ears.
Guzman.   My fury   165
  Is now but justice on thy forfeit life.   *Draws.*
Amoretta. 'Lath, they thall not fight.
Futelli. Fear not, sweet lady.

---

153. He] *Q*; He'll *Weber.*   154. mother-] *This ed.*; mother *Q*; mother's
Weber.   161. Flagon-Draught] *This ed.*; Flagon drought *Q.*   162. harque-
bus] *This ed.*; hargubush *Q.*   167-8.] *Weber; Q prints this as three half-lines.*

---

153. *He blow up*] He'll undermine. Possibly Futelli is speaking pidgin
English for the benefit of Guzman, and so I have not emended.
154. *by his mother-side*] on his mother's side (*OED* mother n.1). The
phrase occurs in *The Rogue* where one of Guzman's Genoese relations
attempts to marry him off to 'his kinswoman by the mother-side' (Alemán
4, p. 21).
155-7.] That the throats did cut of fourteen hundred Dutchmen in one
night ('sneighen' seems to be Ford's rendition of Dutch *snijden*, to cut).
Modern Dutch would give *veertien* and *nacht* for Ford's 'veirteen' and 'neict'.
156. *Hogen Mogen*] Cf. note on 2.1.199.
158.] A half line.
161. *Flagon-Draught*] flagonful.
Snortenfert] Suggestive of 'snort and fart'.
162. *Brogen-foh*] brag and fight.
harquebus] portable gun, which could vary in size from a small cannon to
a musket.
163. *butter-boxes*] boxes for holding butter; used as a derogatory term for
Dutchmen.
164. *jobbernowls*] blockheads.
165. *sconce*] small fort. The phrase is obscure, but the sense is clearly that
the Spanish captured the Dutch stronghold.
165-6. *My … life*] Since you have admitted that you are related to people
who killed Spaniards, your life is forfeit and killing you will be a simple act
of justice.

Piero. [*To Fulgoso and Guzman*] Be advised, great spirits.
Fulgoso. My fortunes bid me to be wise in duels,
    Else hang't, who cares?
Guzman.   Mine honour is my tutor,   170
    Already tried and known.
Futelli.   Why there's the point:
    Mine honour is my tutor too. Noblemen
    Fight in their persons? Scorn't, 'tis out of fashion;
    There's none but hare-brained youths of metal use it.
Piero. Yet put not up your swords: it is the pleasure   175
    Of the fair lady that you quit the field
    With brandished blades in hand.
Futelli.   And more: to show
    Your suffering valour, as her equal favours,
    You both should take a competence of kicks.
Fulgoso, Guzman. How?
Futelli, Piero. Thus and thus. Away, you brace of stinkards.   180
                     [*Futelli and Piero kick them.*]
Fulgoso. Phew, as it were.
Guzman.   Why, since it is her pleasure,
    I dare and will endure it.
Fulgoso.   Phew.
Piero.   Away,
    But stay below.
Futelli.   Budge not, I charge ye,
    Till you have further leave.
Guzman.   Mine honour claims
    The last foot in the field.
Fulgoso.   I'll lead the van then.   *Exit.*   185
Futelli. Yet more? Begone!   [*Exit* GUZMAN.]
    Are not these precious suitors?

---

179. *Fulgoso, Guzman.*] *This ed.*; AMBO *Q.* 181–2. pleasure, / I] *Weber*;
pleasure, I *Q.*

---

    168. *great spirits*] brave souls. Piero addresses Fulgoso and Guzman as if
they were genuine heroes.
    174. *youths of metal*] young men who wear swords, presumably also with
a pun on 'mettle'.
    179. *take a competence of kicks*] have your fair share of being kicked. The
hugely dishonourable act of being kicked puts Fulgoso and Guzman on a par
with other cowardly duellists in Renaissance drama, most notably in *Epicoene.*
    stinkards] people who stink.
    185. *van*] foremost part of an attacking force.

Enter TRELCATIO.

Trelcatio. What tumults fright the house?
Futelli.   A brace of kestrels,
    That fluttered, sir, about this lovely game,
    Your daughter; but they durst not give the souse
    And so took hedge.
Piero.   Mere haggards, buzzards, kites.   190
Amoretta. I thcorn thuch trumpery, and will thape my luff
    Henthforth ath thall my father betht direct me.
Trelcatio. Why now thou singst in tune, my Amoretta,
    And my good friends, you have, like wise physicians,
    Prescribed a healthful diet. I shall think on   195
    A bounty for your pains, and will present ye
    To noble Auria such as your descents
    Commend, but for the present we must quit
    This room to privacy; they come.
Amoretta.   Nay pridee
    Leave me not, dentlemen.
Futelli.   We are your servants.   200
                                  Exeunt.

186.1.] *This ed.; Q has Exit. Enter Trelcatio after l.* 185.   188. fluttered] *Weber*;
flattered *Q*.   190. Mere] *Weber, Gifford, Nogami*; Mee *Q*.   191. trum-
pery] *Gifford (subst.)*; trump[ ] *Q*; trumpe, – and [I] *Weber*.

187. *kestrels*] hunting hawks which flutter over their prey before swooping
down to kill, perhaps also with a play on Kastril in Jonson's *The Alchemist*,
who seeks lessons in how to become a roaring boy.

188. *fluttered*] I have adopted Weber's emendation of Q's 'flattered' in the
interests of modernisation, but 'flattered' is a genuine early variation, found
also in the First Folio text of *Coriolanus* in this context (see Hawkes 53–4
and *OED* flatter, v.2).

189. *souse*] A hunting term. Cf. Juliana Berners, *The booke of hauking,
huntyng and fysshyng, with all the properties and medecynes that are necessary to
be kept*, (London: Robert Toye), 1556: 'If youre hauke nymme the foule a
loft . . . yee wyll saye she tooke it at the mount or at the souce'.

190. *haggards*] young wild hawks, generally female.

buzzards] lesser hawks.

kites] birds of prey belonging to the falcon family.

191. *trumpery*] thing of small value.

thape my luff] direct my course, point my luff (front) sail. This is another
of the play's many sailing metaphors.

[ACT 4 SCENE 3]

Enter AURIA, ADURNI *and* AURELIO.

Auria. You're welcome, be assured you are. For proof,
    Retrieve the boldness, as you please to term it,
    Of visit to commands: if this man's presence
    Be not of use, dismiss him.
Adurni.   'Tis, with favour,
    Of consequence, my lord, your friend may witness   5
    How far my reputation stands engaged
    To noble reconcilement.
Auria.   I observe
    No party here amongst us who can challenge
    A motion of such honour.
Adurni.   Could your looks
    Borrow more clear serenity and calmness   10
    Than can the peace of a composèd soul,
    Yet I presume report of my attempt,
    Trained by a curiosity in youth,
    Forescattering clouds before 'em, hath raised tempests
    Which will at last break out.
Auria.   Hid now, most likely,   15

---

1. You're] *Weber*; Y'are *Q. Weber does not start a new scene at this point.*
10. serenity] *Gifford*; severity *Q.*   14. Forescattering] *This ed.*; For scattering *Q.*

1–4.] As proof that he is genuinely glad to see Adurni and does not consider his visit impertinent, Auria invites him to feel free to manage the situation as he pleases, specifically by asking Aurelio to leave if he does not want him there.

9–15. *Could . . . out*] Well may Auria call this speech 'dark'. As so often with Ford's elliptical, Latinate style, more than one understanding of the syntax is possible. However, I take the gist to be as follows: 'Even if your looks were as sunny and calm as an untroubled person's, I would still assume that the rumour of what I tried to do had raised bad weather, and that your knowledge of it could not remain hidden'.

13.] The construction is ambiguous. Adurni may be saying that his attempt on Spinella was brought on by youthful curiosity, but he may also mean that a report of his doings will have been triggered by the scrutiny habitually applied to the young. The latter is perhaps the likelier interpretation and more in line with the senses in which Ford tends to use 'curiosity', which often carries an overtone of prying or of damagingly close examination.

14. *'em*] Auria's looks.

I'th' darkness of your speech.
Aurelio.   You may be plainer.
Adurni. I shall. My lord, that I intended wrong –
Auria. Ha? Wrong? To whom?
Adurni.   To Auria, and as far
    As language could prevail, did –
Auria.   Take advice,
    Young lord, before thy tongue betray a secret   20
    Concealed yet from the world. Hear and consider:
    In all my flight of vanity and giddiness,
    When scarce the wings of my excess were fledged,
    When a distemperature of youthful heat
    Might have excused disorder and ambition,   25
    Even then, and so from thence till now the down
    Of softness is exchanged for plumes of age
    Confirmed and hardened, never durst I pitch
    On any howsoever likely rest,
    Where the presumption might be constered wrong –   30
    The word is hateful, and the sense wants pardon;
    For as I durst not wrong the meanest, so
    He who but only aimed by any boldness
    A wrong to me should find I must not bear it.

19–36. *Take . . . interruption*] Having even in his youth avoided doing anything that could ever have been construed as a wrong to anyone, Auria would
have to take action if Adurni openly confessed to having wronged him.
Auria's main concern here seems to be to avoid bringing matters to a head,
which an admission that a wrong had been committed would inevitably do.

23.] When the wings which sustained me on my flight of excess had only
just acquired their full plumage (and hence their full capability), i.e. when
my propensity to sow wild oats was just coming into its full strength.

24. *distemperature*] bodily disorder or disturbance.

26. *down*] first feathers of young birds.

27. *plumes*] established plumage of fully-grown birds.

28–9. *pitch . . . rest*] adopt any attitude or mode of behaviour, however
innocuous-seeming.

30. *constered*] construed, understood.

wrong] faulty. Ford inaugurates a sustained playing with the meaning of
the word.

31. *The word is hateful*] The very word 'wrong' is an unpleasant one.

the sense wants pardon] what it connotes is inexcusable.

32. *wrong*] do any disservice to.

34. *wrong*] insult, offence.

bear] swallow, accept.

The one is as unmanly as the other.   35
Now without interruption.
Adurni.   Stand, Aurelio,
And justify thine accusation boldly:
Spare me the needless use of my confession;
And having told no more than what thy jealousy
Possessed thee with again before my face,   40
Urge to thy friend the breach of hospitality
Adurni trespassed in, and thou conceivest
Against Spinella. Why, proofs grow faint
If barely not supposed I'll answer guilty.
Aurelio. You come not here to brave us?
Adurni.   No, Aurelio,   45
But to reply upon that brittle evidence
To which thy cunning never shall rejoin.
I make my judge my jury: be accountant
Whither, with all the eagerness of spleen
Or a suspicious rage can plead, thou hast   50
Enforced the likelihood of scandal.
Aurelio.   Doubt not

43. Why] *Q;* when thy *Gifford.*   49. with all] *Weber;* withall *Q.*   50. Or] *This ed.;* Of *Q.*

43–4. *Why . . . guilty*] Again it is difficult to be sure of the construction. Gifford, noting that l. 43 has only nine syllables, conjectured 'When they' for 'Why' and put commas around 'If barely not suppos'd' to make it a phrase in apposition to 'proofs', but this yields no satisfactory overall sense. The meaning seems rather to be 'Your proof just won't stand up, unless you are imagining that I will confess', but it is hard to explain the 'not'. It is possible that it should be emended to 'but', which would give a sense something like '. . . even if it is considered just credible that I might confess'. Ironically, by pointing out the weakness of the case against him, Adurni is helping Auria in his aim of avoiding confrontation.
   45. *brave*] defy, threaten.
   47. *rejoin*] Ford, who may have spent much of his adult life at the Middle Temple, is here using a legal term meaning to make a reply to a charge. Adurni tells Aurelio that not all his cunning will enable him to make a satisfactory answer once the slimness of the evidence is apparent.
   48. *be accountant*] make reckoning of.
   48–51.] How far you, driven by malice and a suspicious rage, have pushed the idea that there is a scandal here.
   49. *Whither*] to what point.
   spleen] caprice, bad temper.
   51. *Enforced*] driven.

But that I have delivered honest truth,
As much as I believe and justly witness.

Adurni. Loose grounds to raise a bulwark of reproach on.
And thus for that; my errand hither is not   55
In whining truant-like submission,
To cry 'I have offended, pray forgive me,
I will do so no more', but to proclaim
The power of virtue, whose commanding sovereignty
Sets bounds to rebel-bloods and checks; restrains   60
Custom of folly; by example teaches
A rule to reformation; by rewards
Crowns worthy actions and invites to honour.

Aurelio. Honour and worthy actions best beseem
Their lips who practise both and not discourse 'em.   65

Auria. Peace, peace, man; I am silent.

Adurni.   Some there are,
And they not few in number, who resolve
No beauty can be chaste 'less unattempted;
And for because the liberty of courtship
Flies from the wanton on the her comes next,   70

---

60. and checks] *Gifford (subst.)*; and checke *Q*; unchecked *Nogami*.   68. 'less
unattempted] *Weber*; lesse unattempted *Q*; unless attempted *Gifford*.

---

53. *believe*] Aurelio is implicitly conceding that he has not acted from
actual knowledge.

54. *loose grounds*] weak foundations.

bulwark] rampart, fortification.

59. *sovereignty*] rule, power.

60. *Sets . . . checks*] sets bounds and checks to those whose blood incites
them to rebel against constraint.

60–1. *restrains/Custom of folly*] imposes limits to the habits of
foolishness.

62. *rule to reformation*] way to become a reformed character.

64. *beseem*] are appropriate to.

65. *both*] i.e. honour and worthy actions.

67. *resolve*] decide.

68.] an Anglicised version of the Latin tag *Casta est quam nemo rogavit*,
literally 'she is chaste whom no one has asked'.

69. *for because*] seeing that.

liberty] freedom, but perhaps with a play on libertinism, i.e. disregard of
moral restraint.

70. *wanton*] loose woman.

the her] whichever woman.

Meeting ofttimes too many soon seduced,
Conclude all may be won by gifts, by service,
Or compliments of vows; and with this file
I stood in rank. Conquest secured my confidence;
Spinella – storm not, Auria – was an object   75
Of study for fruition; here I angled,
Not doubting the deceit could find resistance.

Aurelio. After confession follows –

Auria.   Noise; observe him.

Adurni. Oh, strange! By all the comforts of my hopes
I found a woman good – a woman good!   80
Yet as I wish belief, or do desire
A memorable mention, so much majesty
Of humbleness and scorn appeared at once
In fair, in chaste, in wise Spinella's eyes
That I grew dull in utterance, and one frown   85
From her could every flame of sensual appetite –

---

86. could] *Q*; cooled *Weber.*

71.] frequently meeting too many (women) who are easily seduced.

72. *service*] courtship.

73. *compliments of vows*] flattering oaths.

73–4. *with ... rank*] I was one of this group. The underlying idea of 'rank and file' refers to the formation of rows and columns in which soldiers stand for drill or to fight.

75. *storm*] rage.

75–6. *object / Of study for fruition*] something to work towards possessing and enjoying.

76. *angled*] fished; hence, intrigued, aimed at.

77.] believing that my trickery would meet no resistance.

78. *Noise; observe him*] Auria cuts off Aurelio, as he did at l. 66, and dismisses his intervention as 'Noise', telling him to listen to what else Adurni has to say. He is obviously confident that if Adurni keeps talking he will clear Spinella.

80.] Adurni's surprise is eloquent testimony to the low esteem in which women are held in the world of the play.

81–2. *desire   /   A   memorable   mention*] want   a   reputation   worth remembering.

84. *fair, chaste, ... wise*] The order in which Adurni lists these attributes, with 'wise' supplying the climax, suggests that he may be beginning to rethink his view of women as merely sex objects. It may also imply that he has detected Auria's wish that he should vindicate Spinella.

86. *could*] Weber's 'cool'd' is ingenious, but if the sentence were thus completed Auria would have no need to ask Adurni not to stop.

Auria. On, sir, and do not stop.
Adurni.   Without protests,
   I pleaded merely love, used not a syllable
   But what a virgin might without a blush
   Have listened to, and not well armed have pitied;   90
   But she, neglecting, cried 'Come, Auria, come
   Fight for thy wife at home!' Then in rushed you, sir;
   Talked in much fury; parted; when as soon
   The lady vanished, after her the rest.
Auria. What followed?
Adurni.   My commission on mine error,   95
   In execution whereof I have proved
   So punctually severe, that I renounce
   All memory, not to this one fault alone,
   But to my other greater and more irksome.
   Now he, whoever owns a name, that consters   100
   This repetition the report of fear,
   Of falsehood, or imposture, let him tell me
   I give myself the lie, and I will clear
   The injury, and man to man, or if

---

95. commission] *Q*; contrition *conj. Gifford.*   101. fear,] *Weber*; fear. *Q.*

90. *armed*] equipped to resist.
91. *neglecting*] ignoring.
93. *parted*] departed.
94. *after her the rest*] everyone else left too.
95. *commission*] Gifford conjectured *contrition*, but Adurni has done what Martino exhorted Levidolce to do at 2.2.80: 'Sit in commission on your own defects', that is, examine your own conduct as if you were a judge.
97. *punctually severe*] exact in every point.
97–9.] I abjure all trace not only of this fault of mine but of all my other, bigger, ones. We do not know what else Adurni may have done, unless he is referring to his previous affair with Levidolce and the subsequent loss of her reputation.
100. *consters*] interprets.
103. *I give myself the lie*] I expose my own falsehood. Anyone who said that Adurni had done this would be implying that he had in effect challenged himself to a duel, since to tell someone they were lying was a standard provocation to single combat.
104–6.] If single combat is considered to be too heavily dependent on individual luck and skill, Adurni is prepared to ask one or more friends of his to fight on his side against any one, two or three opponents who might wish to take him on.

Such justice may prove doubtful, two to two,   105
Or three to three, or any way reprieve
Th'opinion of my forfeit without blemish.
Auria. Who can you think I am? Did you expect
    So great a tameness as you find, Adurni,
    That you cast loud defiance? Say –
Adurni.   I have robbed you   110
    Of rigour, Auria, by my strict self-penance
    For the presumption.
Auria.   Sure Italians hardly
    Admit dispute in questions of this nature.
    The trick is new.
Adurni.   I find my absolution
    By vows of change from all ignoble practice.   115
Auria. Why look ye, friend, I told you this before:
    You would not be persuaded. Let me think.
Aurelio. You do not yet deny that you solicited
    The lady to ill purpose?
Adurni.   I have answered,
    But it returned much quiet to my mind,   120
    Perplexed with rare commotions.
Auria.   That's the way;
    It smooths all rubs.
Aurelio.   My lord?
Auria.   Foh, I am thinking.

---

122. thinking.] *Weber*; thinking *Q*.

106–7. *reprieve ... forfeit*] do anything that will result in my error being pardoned. One might feel that Adurni is rather more concerned with justifying his own reputation than Spinella's, while Aurelio, whose rash action first brought her name into disrepute, is conspicuously silent. Both men could be seen as concerned primarily with protecting their own position, making it clear that Auria, who is genuinely concerned with clearing Spinella's name, faces a difficult task.

109. *tameness*] meekness, submissiveness.

111. *rigour*] severity.

114. *absolution*] pardon.

120.] Adurni has found the act of confession therapeutic.

122. *smooths all rubs*] disposes of all obstacles. The metaphor is from bowling, where a rub is any impediment which prevents a bowl from running its proper course.

You may talk forward – if it take 'tis clear,
And then and then, and so and so.
Adurni.　　　　　　　　　　You labour
　　With curious engines, sure.
Auria.　　　　　　　　Fine ones; I take ye　　　　125
　　To be a man of credit, else –
Adurni.　　　　　　　　Suspicion
　　Is needless; know me better.
Auria.　　　　　　　Yet you must not
　　Part from me, sir.
Adurni.　　　　　For that your pleasure.
Auria.　　　　　　　　　[*Aside*] 'Come,
　　Fight for thy wife at home, my Auria.' Yes,
　　We can fight, my Spinella, when thine honour　　　130
　　Relies upon a champion! Now.

　　　　　　　Enter TRELCATIO.

Trelcatio.　　　　　　　　My lord,
　　Castanna with her sister and Malfato
　　Are newly entered.
Auria.　　　　　[*To Trelcatio*] Be not loud; convey them
　　Into the gallery. [*To the others*] Aurelio, friend,
　　Adurni, lord, we three will sit in council　　　135
　　And piece a hearty league, or scuffle shrewdly.

　　　　　　　　　　　　　　Exeunt.

126–7. Suspicion / Is] *Weber*; suspicion is *Q.*　127–8. not / Part] *Weber*; not
part *Q.*　128–9. Come, / Fight] *Weber (subst.)*; Come fight *Q.*　136.1. *Exeunt*]
Weber; Exit *Q.*

123–4.] Auria dismissively tells Aurelio to talk away while he makes a
private plan.
123. *if it take*] if the idea catches on.
125. *curious engines*] ingenious devices.
126. *man of credit*] man whose word is trustworthy.
131. *Now*] Perhaps a signal to the offstage Trelcatio that the time has come
to announce the arrival of the ladies, since everything is in place for the
denouement.
134.] Auria is effectively escorting all those involved back to the scene of
the 'crime'.
136. *piece*] join together.
hearty] heartfelt.
scuffle shrewdly] have a very good go at it.

Act 5

Enter MARTINO, BENAZZI *and* LEVIDOLCE.

Martino. Ruffian, out of my doors; thou com'st to rob me.
　An officer, what ho! My house is haunted
　By a lewd pack of thieves, of harlots, murderers,
　Rogues, vagabonds; I foster a decoy here,
　And she trolls on her ragged customer　　　　　　　5
　To cut my throat for pillage.
Levidolce.　　　　　　　　Good sir, hear me –
Benazzi. Hear or not hear, let him rave his lungs out! Whiles
　this woman hath abode under this roof, I will justify
　myself her bedfellow in despite of denial; in despite, those
　are my words.　　　　　　　　　　　　　　　　10
Martino. Monstrous!
　Why, sirrah, do I keep a bawdy-house,
　An hospital for panders? O thou monster,
　Thou she-confusion! Are you grown so rampant
　That from a private wanton thou proclaimst thyself　　15
　A baggage for all gamesters, lords, or gentlemen,

ACT 5 [SCENE I].] *This ed.; Actus Quintus. Q.* 7–8.] *Weber; verse in Q.*
11–12. Monstrous! / Why] *Gifford;* Monstrous! why *Q.*

---

3. *lewd*] ignorant and vulgar.
4. *vagabonds*] wastrels.
　foster] care for, nurture.
　decoy] one who lures others into a trap.
5. *trolls*] moves or turns by rolling (*OED* v.2), with a possible pun on
'trulls', meaning prostitutes.
　customer] associate, companion (*OED* n.4a). This is the first of several
suggestions by Martino that Levidolce and Benazzi are no better than a
prostitute and her pimp.
6. *for pillage*] so that they can plunder me.
8–9. *justify myself*] prove that I am.
14. *she-confusion*] female bringer of disaster. The 'she' prefix is inherently
pejorative.
　rampant] unrestrained.
16. *gamesters*] lewd persons, here specifically men.

Strangers, or home-spun yeomen, footposts, pages,
Roarers or hangmen? Hey-day, set up shop,
And then cry a market open, to't, and welcome.
Levidolce. This is my husband.   20
Martino. Husband!
Benazzi. Husband natural; I have married her, and what's
   your verdict on the match, signor?
Martino. Husband, and married her!
Levidolce.   Indeed 'tis truth.
Martino. A proper joining! Give ye joy, great mistress.   25
   Your fortunes are advancèd, marry, are they!
   What jointure is assured, pray? Some three thousand
   A year in oaths and vermin? Fair preferment!
   Was ever such a tattered rag of man's flesh
   Patched up for copesmate to my niece's daughter?   30
Levidolce. Sir, for my mother's name forbear this anger;
   If I have yoked myself beneath your wishes,
   Yet is my choice a lawful one, and I
   Will live as truly chaste unto his bosom
   As e'er my faith hath bound me.
Martino.   A sweet couple!   35

20.] *Weber; verse in Q.*

17. *yeomen*] men of the class below that of gentlemen.
18. *Roarers*] roisterers, revellers.
hangmen] rogues (*OED* hangman 1b).
Hey-day] Oho! Martino sarcastically utters an exclamation which suggests
gaiety and pleased surprise.
18–19. *Hey-day . . . welcome*] Martino is suggesting that Levidolce might
as well offer to prostitute herself to all (male) comers.
22–3.] Benazzi's speech is laid out as two lines of verse in Q, but its
nineteen syllables do not conform to iambic beat, and both his other speeches
in this scene are in prose, something which presumably confirms him as an
outsider to the verse-speaking Martino.
25. *proper joining*] fine coupling.
Give ye joy] congratulations.
27. *jointure*] assignment of lands or money to a wife to maintain her in
the event of her husband's death.
28. *preferment*] advancement, promotion.
30. *copesmate*] marriage partner (*OED* c cites this as a specific instance
of that meaning), but could also mean a paramour or a partner in cheating
and swindling.

Benazzi. We are so. For mine own part, however my outside
   appear ungay, I have wrestled with death, Signor Martino,
   to preserve your sleeps, and such as you are, untroubled.
   A soldier is in peace a mockery, a very town-bull for
   laughter, unthrifts, and landed babies, are prey curmud-   40
   geons lay their baits for; let the wars rattle about your
   ears once, and the security of a soldier is right honourable
   amongst ye then! That day may shine again; so to my
   business.
Martino. A soldier! Thou a soldier! I do believe   45
   Th'art lousy; that's a pretty sign, I grant.
   A villainous poor *bandito* rather, one
   Can man a quean, and cant, and pick a pocket,
   Pad for a cloak, or hat, and in the dark
   Pistol a straggler for a quarter-ducat.   50
   A soldier! Yes, 'a looks as if 'a had not
   The spirit of a herring, or a tumbler.
Benazzi. Let age and dotage rage together! Levidolce, thou
   art mine, on what conditions the world shall soon witness;

---

47. *bandito*] *This ed.*; Bandetti *Q.*

---

   37. *ungay*] shabby.
   39. *town-bull*] bull whose owners take turns at keeping him and who
services all the local cows.
   40. *unthrifts*] ne'er-do-wells.
   landed babies] fools who own land.
   40–1. *are prey . . . baits for*] Benazzi seems to have forgotten that he was
speaking of 'a soldier' in the singular. In peacetime, soldiers are prey for
whom churlish fellows (curmudgeons) set traps.
   45–8.] Martino views Benazzi as a typical ruffian, who whores, steals and
speaks rogues' jargon.
   47. bandito] The original Italian term had not yet become anglicized and
this was the standard form used in England in the period.
   48. *man*] escort (*OED* v.4). Again Martino insinuates that Levidolce is
effectively a prostitute and Benazzi is her pimp.
   quean] prostitute.
   cant] speak the patois of thieves and beggars.
   49. *pad*] follow with intent to steal.
   50.] shoot some night-wanderer for a measly sum.
   52. *tumbler*] someone who lures people into the hands of a swindler (*OED*
2b). In *The Rogue*, Guzman's uncle compares a youth who he thinks falsely
claimed to be related to him (it was actually the young Guzman himself) to
'your tumblers' (Alemán 3, p. 353).

yet since our hands joined, I have not interessed my pos-   55
session of thy bed, nor till I have accounted to thy injunction, do I mean. Kiss me quick and resolute. – So adieu,
signor.

Levidolce. Dear, for love's sake, stay.

Benazzi.   Forbear entreaties. *Exit.*

Martino. Ah, thou – but what? I know not how to call thee;   60
Fain would I smother grief, and out it must.
My heart is broke; thou hast for many a day
Been at a loss, and now art lost for ever –
Lost, lost, without recovery.

Levidolce.   With pardon,
Let me retain your sorrows.

Martino.   'Tis impossible;   65
Despair of rising up to honest fame
Turns all the courses wild, and this last action
Will roar thy infamy. Then you are certainly
Married, forsooth, unto this new-come?

Levidolce.   Yes,
And herein every hope is brought to life   70
Which long hath lain in deadness; I have once more
Wedded Benazzi, my divorcèd husband.

Martino. Benazzi? This the man?

Levidolce.   No odd disguise
Could guard him from discovery; 'tis he,
The choice of my ambition. Heaven preserve me   75
Thankful for such a bounty! Yet he dreams not
Of this deceit, but let me die in speaking
If I repute not my success more happy
Than any earthly blessing. O sweet uncle,
Rejoice with me! I am a faithful convert,   80

---

61. and] *Q*; but *Gifford.*   65. retain] *Q*; restrain *Gifford.*

---

55. *interessed*] taken my right in.

56–7. *accounted to thy injunction*] carried out your command. An injunction is a legal process which restrains the person to whom it is applied from
trespassing on the legal or equitable rights of another.

65. *retain*] hold back.

69. *new-come*] Johnny-come-lately, arriviste.

76. *Yet*] So far.

78–9. *If . . . blessing*] If I do not count the fact that I have been reunited
with Benazzi as a greater blessing than any mere worldly one.

And will redeem the stains of a foul name
By love and true obedience.
Martino.   Force of passion
Shows me a child again. Do, Levidolce;
Perform thy resolutions. Those performed,
I have been only steward for your welfare: 85
You shall have all between ye.
Levidolce.   Join with me, sir;
Our plot requires much speed. We must be earnest:
I'll tell ye what conditions threaten danger,
Unless you intermediate. Let us hasten,
For fear we come too late.
Martino.   As thou intendest   90
A virtuous honesty, I am thy second
To any office, Levidolce witty,
My niece, my witty niece.
Levidolce.   Let's slack no time, sir.

                                                   Exeunt.

[ACT 5 SCENE 2]

Enter TRELCATIO, MALFATO, SPINELLA
and CASTANNA.

Trelcatio. Kinsman and ladies, have a little patience.
All will be as you wish, I'll be your warrant.
Fear nothing: Auria is a noble fellow.
I leave ye, but be sure I am in hearing;
Take courage.   *Exit.*
Malfato.   Courage? They who have no hearts   5
Find none to lose. Ours is as great as his
Who defy danger most. Sure state and ceremony
Inhabit here; like strangers, we shall wait

---

7. defy] *Q* (defie); defies *Weber.*

---

84. *Perform thy resolutions*] Do what you have resolved to.
89. *intermediate*] intervene, act as mediator.
91. *second*] supporter.

2.] I guarantee everything will turn out as you hope.
8–9. *like . . . entertainment*] we shall be kept waiting for a formal reception
as if we were not near kinsfolk.

      Formality of entertainment. Cousin,
      Let us return. 'Tis paltry.
Spinella.   Gentle sir,   10
      Confine your passion; my attendance only
      Commends a duty.
[*Castanna.*]   Now for heaven's sake, sister –

                    Enter AURIA *and* AURELIO.

      'A comes, your husband comes; take comfort, sister.
Auria. Malfato.
Malfato.   Auria.
Auria.   [*Embraces Malfato.*] Cousin, would mine arms
      In their embraces might at once deliver   15
      Affectionately what interest your merit
      Holds in my estimation. I may chide
      The coyness of this intercourse betwixt us,
      Which a retired privacy on your part
      Hath pleased to show. If aught of my endeavours   20
      Can purchase kind opinion, I shall honour
      The means and practice.
Malfato.   'Tis your charity.
Aurelio. Worthy Malfato.
Malfato.   Provident Aurelio.
Auria. Castanna, virtuous maid.
Castanna.   Your servant, brother.
Auria. But who's that other? Such a face mine eyes   25
      Have been acquainted with; the sight resembles
      Something which is not quite lost to remembrance.
                              [*Spinella kneels.*]
      Why does the lady kneel? To whom? Pray rise;
                              [*Spinella rises.*]
      I shall forget civility of manners,
      Imagining you tender a false tribute,   30
      Or him to whom you tender it a counterfeit.

---

12. SP] *Weber; speech prefix missing in Q.*

11–12. *my ... duty*] It is only I who am duty-bound to be here.
31. *counterfeit*] impostor. A favourite Ford word, particularly in *Perkin Warbeck*.

Malfato. My lord, you use a borrowed bravery,
　　Not suiting fair constructions. May your fortunes
　　Mount higher than can apprehension reach 'em,
　　Yet this waste kind of antic sovereignty   35
　　Unto a wife who equals every best
　　Of your deserts, achievements, or posterity
　　Bewrays a barrenness of noble nature.
　　Let upstarts exercise uncomely roughness;
　　Clear spirits to the humble will be humble.   40
　　You know your wife, no doubt.
Auria.　　　　　　　　　Cry ye mercy, gentleman,
　　Belike you come to tutor a good carriage,
　　Are expert in the nick on't; we shall study
　　Instructions quaintly. 'Wife', you said; agreed.
　　Keep fair, and stand the trial.
Spinella.　　　　　　　　Those words raise   45
　　A lively soul in her who almost yielded
　　To faintness and stupidity; I thank ye.
　　Though prove what judge you will, till I can purge
　　Objections which require belief and conscience,

---

37. posterity] *Q*; prosperity *Gifford.*

---

33. *Not suiting fair constructions*] not adapted to a generous interpretation.

35–8.] However, this foolish sort of frivolous demonstration of power over a wife who is your match in merit, achievements and ancestry exposes a shortfall of nobility in your nature. 'Antic', another favourite Ford word, is usually applied to those who fail to show the dignity befitting their position.

38. *Bewrays*] exposes, reveals.

39. *roughness*] aggression, rudeness.

42. *tutor a good carriage*] give lessons in behaviour, but, as Mercutio jokes in *Romeo and Juliet* (1.4.94), carriage can also imply carrying a baby or carrying the weight of a man in bed.

43, 44.] 'nick' and 'quaintly' could both be susceptible of a bawdy double meaning, with 'nick' suggesting the female genitals (*OED* n.2d) and 'quaint' being a variant of 'cunt'. Auria's use of such terms seems to suggest a slur on Spinella, but he then switches direction with the use of the much more respectable term 'wife'.

47. *stupidity*] numbness.

I have no kindred, sister, husband, friend,   50
  Or pity for my plea.
Malfato.   Call ye this welcome?
  We are mistook, Castanna.
Castanna.   O my lord,
  Other respects were promised.
Auria.   Said ye, lady,
  No kindred, sister, husband, friend?
Spinella.   Nor name,
  With this addition: I disclaim all benefit   55
  Of mercy from a charitable thought,
  If one or all the subtleties of malice,
  If any engineer of faithless discord,
  If supposition for pretence in folly,
  Can point out, without injury to goodness,   60
  A likelihood of guilt in my behaviour
  Which may declare neglect in every duty
  Required, fit or exacted.
Auria.   High and peremptory!
  The confidence is masculine.
Malfato.   Why not?
  An honourable cause gives life to truth,   65
  Without control.
Spinella.   I can proceed: that tongue
  Whose venom, by traducing spotless honour,
  Hath spread th'infection, is not more mine enemy
  Then theirs, or his, weak and besotted brains are,
  On whom the poison of its cankered falsehood   70
  Hath wrought for credit to so foul a mischief.
  Speak, sir, the churlish voice of this combustion;
  Aurelio, speak, nor, gentle sir, forbear

---

   63. *peremptory*] dismissive of formalities. In law, peremptory is also a technical term meaning precluding any further discussion. Auria is perhaps reaching for a way of closing the debate.

   64. *The confidence is masculine*] Cf. Vittoria Corombona in Webster's *The White Devil*, who is accused of masculine behaviour when she defends herself in court.

   70. *cankered*] diseased.

   71. *for credit*] to procure belief in.

Aught what you know, but roundly use your eloquence
Against a mean defendant.
Malfato.   He's put to't;   75
It seems the challenge gravels him.
Aurelio.   My intelligence
Was issue of my doubts, not of my knowledge.
A self-confession may crave assistance;
Let the lady's justice impose the penance.
So in the rules of friendship, as of love,   80
Suspicion is not seldom an improper
Advantage for the knitting faster joints
Of faithfulest affection by the fevers
Of casualty unloosed, where lastly error
Hath run into the toil.
Spinella.   Woeful satisfaction   85
For a divorce of hearts.
Auria.   So resolute?
I shall touch nearer home. Behold these hairs,
Great masters of a spirit; yet they are not
By winter of old age quite hid in snow.
Some messengers of time, I must acknowledge,   90
Amongst them took up lodging. When we first
Exchanged our faiths in wedlock, I was proud
I did prevail with one whose youth and beauty

---

79. justice] *Q*; justice [then] *Gifford.*   85–6. satisfaction / For] *Weber*; satisfaction for *Q*.

---

76. *gravels*] perplexes, robs him of speech.
My intelligence] The information I gave.
77.] Arose from what I feared rather than from what I actually knew.
78. *self-confession*] admitting one's own faults.
82–4. *knitting . . . unloosed*] Aurelio suggests that if a happy ending can still be procured it will act like a healing force on a body previously disordered by fever. Implicitly he presents himself, Auria and presumably Spinella as essentially parts of one organic unity.
84. *casualty*] accidental occurrence.
85. *toil*] snare.
88. *Great masters of a spirit*] Horace, *Carminum*, III.xiv.25–6, figures the whitening of the hair as softening the spirit.
90–1.] I must admit that some signs of age have appeared in my hair. The suggestion that Auria is past his first youth strengthens the parallel with Othello (see Introduction, **p. 7**).
91. *took*] have taken.

Deserved a choice more suitable in both.
Advancement to a fortune could not court   95
Ambition either on my side or hers:
Love drove the bargain, and the truth of love
Confirmed it, I conceived; but disproportion
In years amongst the married is a reason
For change of pleasures. Whereto I reply   100
Our union was not forced, 'twas by consent;
So then the breach in such a case appears
Unpardonable. Say your thoughts.
Spinella.   My thoughts
   In that respect are resolute as yours,
   The same; yet herein evidence of frailty   105
   Deserved not more a separation
   Than doth charge of disloyalty objected
   Without or ground or witness. Woman's faults
   Subject to punishments and men's applauded
   Prescribe no laws in force.
Aurelio.   Are ye so nimble?   110
Malfato. A soul sublimed from dross by competition,
   Such as is mighty Auria's famed, descends
   From its own sphere when injuries, profound ones,
   Yield to the combat of a scolding mastery,
   Skirmish of words. Hath your wife lewdly ranged,   115
   Adulterating the honour of your bed?

103–4. thoughts / In] *Weber*; thoughts in *Q*.   104. are resolute] *Gifford*; are
as resolute *Q*.   108. Woman's] *This ed.*; womans *Q*; Women's *Gifford*.
115.] *Gifford*; Skirmish of words hath with your wife lewdly ranged *Q*.

104. *are resolute*] Q's 'are as resolute' is extrametrical and syntactically
unnecessary, so I have followed Gifford's emendation here.
   108. *Without or ground or witness*] Without either reason or testimony.
   108–10. *Woman's . . . force*] No law on the statute book allows for women's
faults to be punished while men's are praised.
   110. *nimble*] full of tricks.
   111. *soul sublimed from dross*] soul from which all baser material has been
purged by chemical (or alchemical) action.
   111–12.] The efforts Auria has made have lifted him above petty
considerations.

Hold dispute, but execute your vengeance
With unresisted rage; we shall look on,
Allow the fact, and spurn her from our bloods;
Else, not detected, you have wronged her innocence   120
Unworthily, and childishly, for which
I challenge satisfaction.
Castanna.   'Tis a tyranny
Over an humble and obedient sweetness
Ungently to insult –

                Enter ADURNI.

Adurni.   That I make good,
And must without exception find admittance   125
Fitting the party who hath herein interest.
Put case I was in fault, that fault stretched merely
To a misguided thought, and who in presence,
Except the pair of sisters fair and matchless,
Can quit an imputation of like folly?   130
Here I ask pardon, excellent Spinella,
Of only you; that granted, he amongst you
Who calls an even reckoning shall meet
An even accountant.
Auria.   Baited by confederacy?
I must have right.
Spinella.   And I, my lord. My lord,   135
What stir and coil is here? You can suspect,
So reconciliation then is needless.
Conclude the difference by revenge, or part,
And never more see one another. Sister,

---

117. Hold] *Q;* Withhold *Gifford;* Hold [not] *Weber.*

   119. *Allow the fact*] admit the crime.
   130. *quit*] clear themselves of.
   132–4.] If anyone but Spinella raises questions about what has happened, Adurni will take him on.
   134. *Baited*] harassed and attacked, like a bear at the stake.
confederacy] conspiracy, preplanned agreement.
   136. *coil*] disturbance.

Lend me thine arm; I have assumed a courage   140
Above my force, and can hold out no longer.
Auria unkind, unkind.   [*Spinella collapses.*]
Castanna.   She faints.
Auria.   Spinella,
Regent of my affections, thou hast conquered.
I find thy virtues as I left them, perfect,
Pure, and unflawed; for instance, let me claim   145
Castanna's promise.
Castanna.   Mine?
Auria.   Yours, to whose faith
I am a guardian, not by imposition,
But by you chosen. Look ye, I have fitted
A husband for you, noble and deserving;
No shrinking back. – Adurni, I present her,   150
A wife of worth.
Malfato.   How's that?
Adurni.   So great a blessing
Crowns all desires of life. The motion, lady,
To me, I can assure you, is not sudden,
But welcomed and forethought. Would you could please
To say the like.
Auria.   Castanna, do. Speak, dearest;   155
It rectifies all crookèd vain surmises.
I prithee speak.

142–3. Spinella, / Regent] *Weber (subst.)*; Spinella, regent *Q.*   156. crookèd]
Gifford; crooks, *Q*; crooks, [all] *Weber.*

140–1. *I . . . force*] I have acted as if I had a courage and strength which I
do not actually possess.

143. *Regent*] ruler.

affections] affections were sometimes distinguished from passions, as when
Shylock says he has 'hands, organs, dimensions, senses, affections, passions'
(*Merchant of Venice* 3.1.56–7), on the grounds that affections were manifesta-
tions of a sensory response while passions were purely emotional. In Ford,
though, 'affection' is the standard term for love: in *The Broken Heart*, for
instance, it is what Penthea feels for Orgilus (2.3.110) and Ithocles for
Calantha (3.5.76), and in *The Lover's Melancholy* it is explicitly said to be
seated in the heart (3.2.117–18). In this play, it is also what Malfato felt for
Spinella (4.1.25).

154. *forethought*] planned in advance.

156.] Adurni's earlier acknowledgement of Spinella's chastity and wisdom
alongside her beauty may have helped prepare the audience to see him as
an acceptable husband for Castanna (4.3.84).

Spinella.   The courtship's somewhat quick,
      The match, it seems, agreed on; do not, sister,
      Reject the use of fate.
Castanna.   I dare not question
      The will of heaven.
Malfato.   Unthought of and unlooked for!   160
Spinella. My ever-honoured lord.
Aurelio.   This marriage frees
      Each circumstance of jealousy.
Auria.   Make no scruple,
      Castanna, of the choice; 'tis firm and real.
      Why else have I so long with tameness nourished
      Report of wrongs, but that I fixed on issue   165
      Of my desires? Italians use not dalliance
      But execution; herein I degenerated
      From custom of our nation, for the virtues
      Of my Spinella rooted in my soul,
      Not common form of matrimonial compliments,   170
      Short lived, as are their pleasures. Yet in sooth,
      My dearest, I might blame your causeless absence,
      To whom my love and nature were no strangers;
      But being in your kinsman's house, I honour
      His hospitable friendship, and must thank it.   175
      Now lasting truce on all hands.
Aurelio.   You will pardon
      A rash and over-busy curiosity.
Spinella. It was to blame, but the success remits it.
Adurni. Sir, what presumptions formerly have grounded
      Opinion of unfitting carriage to you,   180

---

170. Not] *This ed.*; Yet *Q*; The *Weber; missing line conj. Gifford.*

169–70.] Gifford conjectured that there was a line missing here, since
without emendation the phrase 'common form of matrimonial pleasures' is
syntactically disconnected from any other part of the sentence. Sense can
perhaps just about be extracted with minimal emendation ('Not' for 'yet') if
we assume Auria to be explaining that his behaviour has been governed by
a conviction of Spinella's virtue. It was this which had taken root in his soul
rather than the 'common form of matrimonial compliments': if he had been
governed by that 'common form' alone, which is inherently ephemeral, he
would not have been so steadfast.
      178. *success*] happy outcome.
      remits it] procures its pardon.

    On my part I shall faithfully acquit
    At easy summons.
Malfato.   You prevent the nicety;
    Use your own pleasure –

      Enter BENAZZI, *his sword drawn,* LEVIDOLCE *and*
             MARTINO *following.*

Aurelio.   What's the matter?
Auria.   Matter?
Benazzi. Adurni and Malfato found together!
    Now for a glorious vengeance.
Levidolce.   Hold, oh, hold him!   185
Aurelio. This is no place for murder, yield thy sword.
[*Auria.*] Yield it, or force it; set you up your shambles
    Of slaughter in my presence?
Adurni.   Let him come.
              [*Auria disarms Benazzi.*]
Malfato. What can the ruffian mean?
Benazzi.   I am prevented.
    The temple, or the chamber of the duke,   190
    Had else not proved a sanctuary. Lord,
    Thou hast dishonourably wronged my wife.
Adurni. Thy wife! I know not her, nor thee.
Auria.   [*To Spinella and Castanna*] Fear nothing.
Levidolce. Yes, me you know. Heaven has a gentle mercy
    For penitent offenders. Blessèd ladies,   195
    Repute me not a castaway, though once
    I fell into some lapses, which our sex
    Are oft entangled by; yet what I have been
    Concerns me now no more, who am resolved
    On a new life. This gentleman, Benazzi,   200

---

187. *Auria*] *Weber; Aure. Q.*

181–2. *acquit . . . summons*] Now it is Adurni's turn to deploy legal termi-
nology, perhaps indicating his growing integration into the community.
182. *You prevent the nicety*] You forestall the need for scruple.
189–91. *I . . . sanctuary*] If he had not been forestalled, Benazzi would
have carried out his threat even in church, like Laertes in *Hamlet* (4.7.125),
or in the Duke's own room. Given that he presumably recognises his former
employer Auria and may know that Auria will need soldiers in Cyprus, it is
perhaps good policy to advertise his fierceness.

Disguisèd as you see, I have re-married.
I knew you at first sight, and tender constantly
Submission for all errors.
Martino.   Nay, 'tis true, sir.
Benazzi. I joy in the discovery, am thankful
Unto the change.
Auria.   Let wonder henceforth cease,   205
For I am partner with Benazzi's counsels,
And in them was director. I have seen
The man do service in the wars late past
Worthy an ample mention; but of that
At large hereafter. Repetitions now   210
Of good or bad would straiten time presented
For other use.
Martino.   Welcome, and welcome ever.
Levidolce. [*To Benazzi*] Mine eyes, sir, never shall without
          a blush
Receive a look from yours. [*To all*] Please to forget
All passages of rashness; such attempt   215
Was mine, and only mine.
Malfato.   You have found a way
To happiness; I honour the conversion.
Adurni. Then I am freed.
Malfato.   May style your friend your servant.
Martino. Now all that's mine is theirs.
Adurni.   But let me add
An offering to the altar of this peace. [*Gives them a purse.*]   220
Auria. How likes Spinella this? Our holy day
Deserves the calendar.
Spinella.   This gentlewoman
Reformed must in my thoughts live fair and worthy;

***

211. *straiten*] constrict.
220. Presumably Adurni gives Levidolce and Benazzi a purse at this point. Gifford thought that Spinella and Castanna also gave her money, but it seems equally likely that it is simply acknowledgement that they bestow, and for which she thanks them.
222. *calendar*] The date is worthy of being recorded in the list of special dates.

    Indeed you shall.

Castanna.   And mine; the novelty
    Requires a friendly love.

Levidolce.   You are kind and bountiful.   225

Enter TRELCATIO, FUTELLI, AMORETTA, PIERO,
driving in FULGOSO *and* GUZMAN.

Trelcatio. By your leaves, lords and ladies, to your jollities
    I bring increase with mine too. Here's a youngster
    Whom I call son-in-law, for so my daughter
    Will have it.

Amoretta.   Yeth in sooth thee will.

Trelcatio.   Futelli
    Hath weaned her from this pair.

Piero.   Stand forth, stout lovers.   230

Trelcatio. Top and topgallant pair; and for his pains,
    She will have him, or none. He's not the richest
    I'th parish, but a wit; I say Amen,
    Because I cannot help it.

Amoretta.   'Tith no matter.

Auria. We'll remedy the penury of fortune: 235
    They shall with us to Corsica. Our cousin
    Must not despair of means, since 'tis believed
    Futelli can deserve a place of trust.

Futelli. You are in all unfellowed.

Amoretta.   Withely thpoken.

Piero. Think on Piero, sir.

Auria.   Piero, yes,   240
    But what of these two pretty ones?

Fulgoso.   I'll follow
    The ladies, play at cards, make sport and whistle;
    My purse shall bear me out. A lazy life
    Is scurvy, and debauched; fight you abroad,
    And we'll be gaming, whiles you fight, at home.   245

---

230. pair] *Gifford*; paine *Q.*   245. gaming] *Gifford*; game *Q.*

229. *thee*] Amoretta's lisped version of 'she'.
231. *Top and topgallant*] with all sail set, in full career (see also note on
2.1.54).
239. *unfellowed*] without equal, peerless.
243. *My purse shall bear me out*] Money will see me through.

Run high, run low, here is a brain can do't.
But for my martial brother don, prithee make him
A what-d'ee-call't, a setting dog, a sentinel;
I'll mend his weekly pay.
Guzman.   He shall deserve it.
Vouchsafe employment honourable.
Fulgoso.   Marry,   250
The don's a generous don.
Auria.   Unfit to lose him.
Command doth limit us short time for revels;
We must be thrifty in them. None, I trust,
Repines at these delights; they are free and harmless.
After distress at sea, the danger's o'er;   255
Safety and welcomes better taste ashore.

EPILOGUE.

The court's on rising; 'tis too late
To wish the lady in her fate
Of trial now more fortunate.
A verdict in the jury's breast
Will be given up anon at least;   5
Till then 'tis fit we hope the best.
Else if there can be any stay,
Next sitting without more delay,
We will expect a gentle day.

---

246. *Run high, run low*] However the dice fall; a reference to a game played with loaded dice, sometimes called 'high men and low men' (see Ben Jonson, *Every Man in His Humour* 3.1.474–5).

248. *setting dog*] dog trained to 'set' (reveal the location of) game in hunting.

1. *The court's on rising*] the court is about to rise from its session.

3. *trial*] Another legal reference.

more fortunate] This presumably refers to the play's reception rather than to the outcome for Spinella, which could hardly have been improved.

4. *verdict in the jury's breast*] The audience must act as jury and decide what they feel about the play.

7. *stay*] suspension of a judicial proceeding.

8. *sitting*] session of the court.

9. *gentle day*] happy outcome.

Index